WHAT THE CHURCH HAS
HIDDEN FROM US . . .

BUT WHAT GOD IS
NOW REVEALING

Russ Miner

ACKNOWLEDGMENTS

I sincerely appreciate my wife and life's companion, Gray, who not only encouraged the writing of this book, but also provided substantive textual input, editing and proofing. She has been a resource in so many ways.

I want to thank the following, who either directly or indirectly have assisted in my biblical/historical education and spiritual growth. They are listed alphabetically.

- Ramon Bennett is a Jerusalem author whose excellent books concerning Israel and the Middle East situation provided great help in understanding the truth of what is really happening there. We were the U.S. distributor of his books for five years.
- Bridges For Peace is an Israel support organization that has produced a large amount of material on the history of Christianity and Judaism.
- Christian Friends of Israel is an Israel support organization which my wife and I had the pleasure of working for in Jerusalem. Its dedication to Israel and the Jewish people is infectious, and spurred us on.
- Beverly Clapp leads a Messianic fellowship in Cave Junction, Oregon. Her discussions concerning our Hebrew roots opened our eyes to truth.
- First Fruits of Zion developed the HaYesod (The Foundation) program — an excellent series of lessons on Hebrew roots. I had the pleasure of leading several Bible studies using this

material. We also had the privilege of doing some editing and proofing of HaYesod before publication in their Jerusalem offices.

- Larry and Martha Freeman, our next-door neighbors whom Yahweh graciously put us next to in 1994, have provided important insights through personal discussions and Bible studies. Martha is also thanked for reviewing the final draft.
- Dr. John Garr's excellent books, articles, and input at conferences on the Hebrew roots of the Christian faith have been very helpful and are frequently quoted.
- Dave Hunt has written excellent books on a variety of topics. His material on Catholicism was instrumental in opening my eyes to the need for carefully studying the history of the religion.
- Zola Levitt's publications on a variety of topics, especially anti-Semitism, have been very helpful.
- Pastor John Long, who leads a Tulelake (California) Fellowship, and his wife Diana have been an inspiration to my wife and me in our Bible studies of the weekly Torah readings.
- United Evangelical Free Church (UEFC) and Pastor Robin Maxson allowed me to lead Bible studies in the church on Hebrew roots and Yahweh's (God's) Leviticus 23 appointments.
- Marvin Wilson's input through his book, *Our Father Abraham*, and at conferences has been an important resource concerning the Hebrew roots of Christianity.

TABLE OF CONTENTS

PREFACE

The "institution of the church" has covered up many *biblical truths* during the past 1900 years. Most of this occurred during the 100-500 AD period, when *biblical* Christianity was changed in many ways by early "church fathers" after Yeshua (Jesus) and the disciples had departed. However, much of the paganism brought into biblical Christianity by the early fathers was still carried forward by the church even after the 16th century Protestant Reformation.

This work discusses how and why the church chose to hide significant truths from its followers. I should make it clear that individual Christians are not the target of this critique, because we are the victims. The "institution" has unfortunately been very successful in hiding these things – keeping us from seeing fundamentally significant *biblical truth*.

I started seeing where *biblical Christianity* differs from the "institution of Christianity" about six years ago, after visits to Israel. I was prompted to start *carefully* studying what the Bible really says and compare it to history. Unfortunately, *biblical Christianity* has been changed and distorted by the church in some very significant ways. This work is an attempt to reveal how and why these changes and distortions occurred.

It has been very difficult to write something that is critical of a system that has been the main part of my family's life for so many years. Our children were raised in the tradition of the "institution of the church", and they presently are raising their families in the same way. They are understandably perplexed because we are challenging the institution in which we raised them. I hope that this book will provide an appropriate explanation for them, and Christian friends, as to why this needs to be done.

My wife, Gray, and I have been in a dilemma – should *we now* cover up and ignore the biblical truths that have become known to us in the last six years, or should we *reveal* these unsettling things that we have learned about the church? Should we remain warm and comfy within the church institution, or live with the discomfort of exposing where things went wrong?

I believe that Yahweh (God) is leading me to add another voice to the chorus of exposing how the Christian system has been taken off track, no matter what the personal consequences are. I frankly have not enjoyed the looks or skepticism, and sometimes derision, as I have tried from time to time to explain different "pieces" of the story to Christian friends and family. This piecemeal approach simply hasn't worked, and it certainly has not been a helpful step toward winning friends and influencing people either.

As a consequence, it seems me that the alternative is to try and put all the "pieces" on the table at the same time and show how they fit together – something akin to a giant complex jigsaw puzzle. And, it is amazing that they do fit together. Many Christians will strongly resist the conclusions of this book. If so, they will need to take this up with Yahweh, because I am only a messenger relating what He has clearly said in His Bible. I have tried very hard to let the Bible speak for itself, and minimize "interpretations".

As I have researched history and studied the Bible, I have become more and more angered and frustrated that *the church did in fact hijack biblical Christianity*, turning into a religion that is part biblical and part pagan. I have tried to control this anger, but it leaks out as sarcasm in the writing from time to time, and I ask for your tolerance of this. However, the anger is tempered somewhat because I personally know many Christians, including family and friends, who have a close relationship with Yeshua and are growing spiritually, in spite of what the "institution of church" has done. Yahweh continues to do a work in many lives.

I often reflect on how Hitler, in *less than a decade* of lies and deceit, was able to mesmerize the German people into believing that for the good of mankind the Jews must be exterminated. He nearly succeeded in doing this outrageous thing. And then I think about how the church has had *centuries* to perfect its own set of lies and deceits in leading Christians away from true biblical Christianity. The analogy here focuses on **length of time only**, and makes no inference that the church is in any way similar to Hitler.

Unless Yahweh is willing to intervene and create a miracle, most Christians will not read this book when they see the bottom line, because the immediate reaction will be one of shock and total disbelief. The church has mesmerized us too well. But I continue to pray that He *will* intervene.

In spite of these negative thoughts, my hope still remains that a thoroughly documented synthesis of biblical truth *along with* credible historical analysis is something that people will read, even if they end up disagreeing with the findings and conclusions. Regardless of where you, the reader, stand in your relationship to Yahweh (God) and Yeshua (Jesus), I encourage you to read it with as an objective and open mind as possible.

Finally, nothing herein is intended to imply or suggest that my own walk with Yahweh and Yeshua is at some higher level than other believers. If anything, coming to understand what the *biblical walk really is* has brought into sharp focus how deficient I am in many areas, and has shown me where I need to grow spiritually. This book is simply an attempt to define biblical truth and standards, and has nothing to do with my successes and failures at meeting these standards.

I have no agenda, no reputation to protect, and no pride of authorship. If there are any errors, I want to know about them. Please send any comments – positive or negative – to me at PO Box 846, Keno, OR 97627.

1. INTRODUCTION & OVERVIEW

(The entire Glossary, at the end of the book, should be reviewed now and during the reading because definitions/meanings of terms are critically important)

The overall thesis of this book could be briefly stated in the following way. In the early centuries, after Yeshua (Jesus) and the apostles were gone, the path that Yahweh (God) and Yeshua had carefully laid out for the Christian church to follow was significantly changed by a group of men, the early "church fathers", who thought they had a better way. They blended pagan traditions from a competing religion, Mithraism, with the *biblical Christianity* (see Glossary) of Yahweh and Yeshua, forcing it off the planned path. They intentionally worked to separate Christianity from Judaism, creating a quantum leap in anti-Semitism as they did so. This separation has continued to grow for nearly 1900 years, but in the present day Yahweh is acting to close the gap — to heal the relationship — between Judaism and Christianity. This will require, among other things, that the church return completely to the *true biblical Christianity* of Yahweh and Yeshua.

For the most part, the pagan rites and traditions that were blended with *biblical* Christianity during the 2nd through 5th centuries were successfully disguised and hidden by the church, but much of this early blending still exists to this day, and significant problems remain in the church's core beliefs and the ways in which it worships. The separation that resulted has created virulent anti-

Semitism, which in turn has led the church to reject the spiritual applications of the Hebrew Scriptures/Torah (Glossary). And, rejection of the Torah has further led to the church's complete misunderstanding of the *joy* that Yahweh had intended for *all* believers, particularly with respect to His Sabbath and appointments in Leviticus Chapter 23.

However, Yahweh is moving to reveal truths that have been covered up, truths that have been hidden for centuries, and which will lead to the future restoration of Judaism and Christianity. Perhaps soon, He will cause the Jews and the Christians to be *reunited* in accordance with biblical prophecies implicit in Ezekiel 37, Matthew 23:37-39 and Ephesians 2:14-18. We are now starting to see the beginning of "the restoration of all things" (Acts 3:21).

By way of definition, "Yeshua" is Jesus' Hebrew name – the one His mother would have used. "Yeshua" derives from the original Hebrew form "Yehoshuah", which means "Yahweh is Salvation". God named Himself "YHWH"(the Hebrew Tetragrammaton) in Exodus 3:14-15, and these letters become "Yahweh" when vowels are added.

FURTHER UNVEILING OF THE PROBLEMS

Fortunately, even with the negatives highlighted above, there are still many aspects of *biblical Christianity* that are being faithfully followed by the "church" (see Glossary) today. This is good news, but at the same time, doing many things correctly has also *covered up many deviations* from the true biblical path. The New Testament is being followed by sincere Christians in many respects, but this has also provided a cover for a number of pagan traditions that have been mixed with *true biblical* Christianity. We can still be very thankful that there are many Christians who have personal relationships with Yahweh and Yeshua, despite the areas in which the church is guilty of hiding biblical truth. It also needs to be stated up front that this work is not a rebuke of individual Christians, but it is a challenge to the "institution of church" to *return totally to the true biblical path and teach Christians accordingly.*

The deviations from the biblical course have included both

following worship patterns not in the Bible, and not following teachings and instructions that are clearly in it. Unfortunately, the Protestant Reformation in the 1500's only went part way in reducing the damage that had been done earlier. The Reformation eliminated some of the unbiblical worship methods that had been instituted, but it still failed to bring about obedience to many of Yahweh's teachings and instructions in the Torah that had been rejected earlier. It will be shown that vicious anti-Semitism, still existing after the Reformation, produced a church that has continued to reject spiritual applications of the Hebrew Scriptures/Torah to this day.

Most Christians are unaware that they are presently worshipping Yeshua and Yahweh through many traditions that have been forced on the Bible by man. We have been blinded from knowing that some important Bible commands are still very much in force, but we have been led to believe that they no longer needed to be observed or followed. Similarly, we have been blinded to the fact that new *unbiblical* commands have been added, and yet we follow them without question.

Yahweh is, in this present time, revealing to Christian believers the truth of how early Christianity was taken off course. There is strong evidence from around the world that Christians are returning to their Hebrew roots and starting to question past deceptions. He wants to remove the cover-up that has been in place for nearly 1900 years. He is revealing in this day what the church has hidden from us as we approach the end of the present age (Glossary) and await Yeshua's return.

This work offers no new or startling ways to interpret controversial Bible passages, nor does it try to develop some exciting new theory. It is simply an analysis of the various issues and problems that the church has been hiding for the last 1900 years, and that have been written about extensively by many others. However, it does offer one possible advancement: A synthesis that clearly shows how *all* these issues relate to each other and fit together. Such a synthesis has not been found in the literature.

People from all different perspectives – academicians, biblical scholars, pastors and lay people (e.g., the author) – need to illuminate Bible truth. As Christians learn the truth about the past problems and cover-ups, it seems that they should become vocal in pointing them out. The pressure needs to be increased and applied relentlessly. The present work is an attempt to provide a warning and wake-up call to the church.

LITERAL INTERPRETATION OF THE BIBLE

Great care has been taken to base findings/conclusions strictly on the Bible; that is, reading it literally and letting it interpret itself. At this point, it would be well to take some space and expand on this statement. We need to see clearly at the outset exactly *why* the Bible can be fully relied on.

Fulfilled prophecy is the vehicle that is used here to show that the Bible is true. There are many reasons that demonstrate why the Bible is the true Word of Yahweh (God), but studying fulfilled prophecy is an easy to understand and eye-opening way to do so.

The Bible can be literally read and interpreted because it is His inspired, supernatural Word. It is supernatural in that it contains around 1000 prophetic passages (about one third of the Bible), and nearly half of these have already been fulfilled *LITERALLY*. These fulfillments are exact in every detail, and such exactness could have come only from someone who is all-knowing, all-seeing, and all-powerful. A person does not have to be an expert in theology or anything else to understand that Yahweh is the one and only God – all he needs to do is read the Bible and examine fulfilled prophecy.

Further, over 200 of the fulfilled prophecies give specific details surrounding Yeshua's first coming, all of which were *LITERALLY* fulfilled in exact detail. Many Bibles include the major prophecies that show that the Messiah of Israel is fulfilled in Yeshua. The majority of the remaining fulfilled prophecies deal with the restoration of Israel that has been unfolding since she was reborn in 1948 and continues in the present day. We know that all of these amazing fulfillments could only have come under Yahweh's superintendence. He is the creator and sustainer of the universe. If there is any doubt whatsoever that Yahweh is the one and only God of our universe and that Yeshua is His one and only Son, you are encouraged at this point to quickly review the examples of fulfilled prophecy in Chapter 7.

We can rely completely on His Word. We can read future history in the Bible – only the exact *TIMING* of future events has not been made known to us. However, we can know the "season" in which we are living by carefully watching how the unfolding of world events aligns with Bible prophecy. For example, consider the early passages of Matthew 24, where Yeshua describes the coming end times (unless noted otherwise, Scripture references are from the New King James Version):

> (4) And Jesus answered and said to them: "Take heed that no one deceives you. (5) For many will come in My name, saying, 'I am the Christ', and will deceive many. (6) And you will hear of wars and rumors of wars. See that you are not troubled; for all these things must come to pass, but the end is not yet. (7) For nation will rise against nation, and kingdom against kingdom. And there will be famines, pestilences, and earthquakes in various places. (8) All these are the beginning of sorrows."

Nation rising against nation, wars, rumors of war, famine, and earthquakes are occurrences that we see happening with increasing frequency and intensity. The labor pains are coming closer together. We have entered the "season" of the end times. "The beginning of sorrows" has arrived.

DIFFERENCES BETWEEN THE PRE-MILLENNIAL AND OTHER VIEWS

A literal reading and interpretation of the Bible is known as the Pre-Millennial view, in which two of the major events are Yeshua's second coming that starts the 1000 year Millennium and the restoration of Israel. Readers who identify with the Amillennial view (there is no Millennium and the church replaced Israel) and the Post-Millennial view (we are presently in the Millennium and the church has replaced Israel) will frankly not understand or agree with much of the discussion in this book, because these two views do not interpret the Bible literally.

For example, *The Essential Catholic Handbook* states: "This belief (in the Millennium) is based on a reading of the Book of Revelation, especially Chapter 20. The (Catholic) Church has rejected this literal interpretation of the text." (1) (See Chapter Notes) The Amillennial and Post-Millennial views frequently allegorize (change the biblical meaning of) numerous passages of Scripture. Many of these passages are interpreted so that the church has replaced Israel and that there is no future Millennium. These views generally do not allow literal interpretation of "apocalyptic" passages (which are found mainly in Revelation and the books of the prophets). Examine the brief introduction to Chapter 4 right now if you would like to see the terrible results of what happened in the early centuries of the church as a result of allegorizing Scripture.

Both views hold that Christianity replaced Israel after Rome had destroyed Jerusalem in the wars of 70 and 135 AD, scattering the Jewish people around the world. They do not accept the many passages that clearly describe the Millennium, nor do they accept the numerous passages which predict Israel's scattering and later restoration to the land, as is now occurring. Readers who associate with the Amillennial and Post-Millennial views are encouraged to read on so that they might better understand the Pre-Millennial view.

Here are a few illustrations of *literal* interpretation. In the following passage, Acts 1:6, Yeshua affirms that the kingdom of Israel will be restored. He says that we will not know the time of Israel's future *literal restoration*, but confirms that it will be restored *by the way* that He answered the question.

> [6]Therefore, when they had come together, they asked Him, saying, "Lord, will You at this time restore the kingdom to Israel?" [7]And He said to them, "It is not for you to know times or seasons which the Father has put in His own authority."

Yeshua confirms that the "kingdom" will be restored to "Israel", which literally refers to that piece of land on the east coast of the

Mediterranean Sea that Yahweh promised to the descendants of Abraham-Isaac-Jacob. "Israel" is most definitely not the "church", and the Bible never says or implies in any way that the "church" has replaced Israel.

In the following passage, Ezekiel 36:24-28, Yahweh gives a promise, repeated numerous times in the Bible, clearly stating that *Israel will be restored to the land of Israel:*

> 24For I will take you from among the nations, gather you out of all countries, and bring you into your own land. 25Then I will sprinkle clean water on you, and you shall be clean; I will cleanse you from all your filthiness and from all your idols. 26I will give you a new heart and put a new spirit within you; I will take the heart of stone out of your flesh and give you a heart of flesh. 27I will put My Spirit within you and cause you to walk in My statutes, and you will keep My judgments and do *them.* 28Then you shall dwell in the land that I gave to your fathers; you shall be My people, and I will be your God.

Zechariah 14:3-4 clearly shows the return of Yeshua when He stands on the Mount of Olives at the end of the battle of Armageddon: 3Then the LORD will go forth and fight against those nations, as He fights in the day of battle. 4 And that day His feet will stand on the Mount of Olives, which faces Jerusalem on the east. And the Mount of Olives shall be split in two, from east to west . . .

Revelation 19:11-14 clearly shows Yeshua's return from heaven to earth, followed by all His saved people, "the armies of heaven", who have been there with Him:

> 11Now I saw heaven opened, and behold, a white horse. And He who sat on him *was* called Faithful and True, and in righteousness He judges and makes war. 12His eyes *were* like a flame of fire, and on His head *were* many crowns. He had a name written that no one knew except Himself. 13He *was* clothed with a robe dipped in blood, and His name is called The Word of God. 14And the armies in heaven, clothed in fine linen, white and clean, followed Him on white horses.

We can have complete confidence that the above prophecies will be fulfilled exactly as written because nearly half of the Bible's prophecies *have already been fulfilled exactly as written.* However, Amillennial and Post-Millennial views would allegorize, or spiritualize, these passages in such a way that the interpretations support the conclusions that the church has replaced Israel and that there is no future Millennium.

OVERVIEW OF TOPICS TO BE DISCUSSED

Our journey will begin early in the 2nd century, after Yeshua and the apostles were gone, and church history will carefully be examined from that point through the 5th century. It will be shown how and why, under control of the early "church fathers", Christianity became separated from its Hebraic roots (and Judaism). A competitor religion, Mithraism, further influenced this separation, and out of Mithraism came many of the pagan rites that the early "fathers" mixed into biblical Christianity.

The next topic is Yeshua's relationship to His only Bible, the Hebrew Scriptures/Torah (Old Testament). We need to see that there are many spiritual applications in the Torah for Christians in this day. *Perhaps the pivotal finding of this book is that the word "Torah" in the Hebrew Scriptures was mistranslated to become just "law" in our English Bibles; "Torah" also includes Yahweh's teachings and instructions.* The validity of this statement will be demonstrated in several different ways in Chapter 4. We will also consider the unfortunate consequences that have resulted from the church's rejection of Yahweh's teachings that are embedded throughout the Hebrew Scriptures.

The focus will then be on Yahweh's divine appointments outlined in Leviticus 23 to see what meaning there is for us today. These are *HIS* appointments that He makes with *everyone* who follows *biblical* Christianity. They include the Sabbath and His three appointments at the time of Passover in the spring, Feast of Weeks (Pentecost) in the summer, and the three appointments taking place around the time of the Day of Atonement in the fall. We will examine passages on the Sabbath from the Hebrew

Scriptures and New Testament that demonstrate how important observing the Sabbath (7th day) is to Yahweh. These divine appointments would not have been discarded by the church if it had not rejected the Torah.

It will be shown that the three spring appointments commemorate Yeshua's first coming (His death, burial, and resurrection), and the three fall appointments point to events surrounding His second coming (the "caught up", His physical return to earth, and the Millennium). Again, see the Glossary for definition of the "caught up".

Finally, the restoration of Israel is discussed — that which has already occurred and that which Yahweh will soon complete. First is an examination of the fulfilled prophecies concerning the remarkable restoration of the Jewish people to the land of Israel. After this, we will see that the Bible also says many gentile Christians will be returning to the land as part of this restoration process.

By carefully analyzing these issues through the eyes of the Bible and history, we will see precisely *"WHAT THE CHURCH HAS HIDDEN FROM US . . . BUT WHAT YAHWEH IS NOW REVEALING"*.

"NOW REVEALING"? Yes, when Israel was reborn as a nation in 1948 numerous prophecies in the Bible started to make sense and to become clearer. Recall that Yahweh told Daniel that His prophecies would not be understandable until the end times. Daniel 12:4,8-9 says:

> 4"But you, Daniel, shut up the words, and seal the book until the time of the end; many shall run to and fro, and knowledge shall increase.". . . 8Although I heard, I did not understand. Then I said, "My lord, what *shall be* the end of these *things?*" 9And he said, "Go *your way,* Daniel, for the words *are* closed up and sealed till the time of the end.

"The time of the end" has arrived, many are running "to and fro", and Yahweh *is now revealing* many things that have been hidden, not only from a prophetic standpoint concerning Israel, but also because He is now bringing His church completely back to the true biblical course.

The Jews through the centuries have preserved the Hebrew Scriptures/Torah, but have been guilty of not believing in Yeshua; on the other hand, the church believes in Yeshua, but has been guilty of rejecting the Hebrew Scriptures/Torah. Of course, there are exceptions in both groups. At the future point in time when the Jews have accepted Yeshua as their Messiah, and the church has accepted the spiritual aspects of the Hebrew Scriptures/Torah, the unity prophecied in Ephesians 2 and Ezekiel 37, which is discussed in Chapter 8, will be achieved and Yeshua will return. This is the reunion pictured on the front cover.

POTENTIAL AUDIENCES FOR THIS BOOK

You, the individual believer, are the primary audience for this work. You are likely to be dismayed, or in a state of disbelief, as deceptions in the church's past are exposed to light. You may decide to not read this book for fear of what you might find, and this of course is your right. However, please realize that we are approaching the end of this age, and Yahweh will be using many different ways to inform us of His truths. He will prevail – one way or another. Perhaps now is the time to get serious about seeing Bible truths that the "institution of church" has hidden. Remember – this book is not a rebuke of individual Christians, but it is a challenge of the "institution of church".

The individual believer usually has no agenda to maintain, nor does his job depend on what he believes or how he worships, so he is able to accept and work with truth. On the other hand, the mainline Protestant denominations, the Catholic Church, the seminaries and other religious institutions have a vested interest in seeing to it that the church's foundations not be disturbed. They continue to find it necessary to ignore biblical truth and history.

Individual Jewish and non-Jewish believers in Yeshua should find this book of interest because it bears on critical historical and current-day issues concerning Judaism and Christianity. Even though you will encounter challenges to what you have been taught, please realize that what you read here comes directly from the Bible and authentic historical sources.

It also could be of interest to unbelievers who are in the process of considering a personal relationship with Yeshua. Even for unbelievers who are not planning on such a relationship, they will see that Yahweh is indeed the God of this universe, and that through His one and only Son, Yeshua, we have our only hope for eternal life and forgiveness of sin. Historians are likely to be interested in the early chapters dealing with church and biblical history.

It is important to state that nothing herein is intended to detract in any way from the salvation and eternal life that a believer has received after making a true heart acceptance of Yeshua as Lord and Savior. This is not a discussion about salvation issues. This work is an attempt to draw believers back to a lifestyle and belief system that faithfully follows the biblical Christianity that Yeshua and the apostles carefully established.

2. SEPARATION OF CHRISTIANITY AND JUDAISM

After Yeshua was crucified, His disciples and other followers continued to spread the Christian faith. The Book of Acts and many of Paul's letters show that Christianity moved to the west and north from Israel as it spread to other nations during the latter part of the first century and into the second century. Unfortunately, during the period 100-500 AD, negative forces were acting to separate Christianity from her mother, Judaism.

THE FIRST CENTURY JERUSALEM CHURCH

Before starting the story of how and why Christianity and Judaism separated, it is important to see the unity that had existed between the two in the beginning. The glorious picture of this unity has been captured by the recent archeological discovery of the first century Judeo-Christian Synagogue on Mount Zion. In this synagogue was found the Messianic Seal of the Jerusalem Church, which had re-emerged after nearly 2000 years of burial.

The Seal is shown on the book's cover, which depicts the unity of the Jerusalem Church in the first century. The cover then shows that for the next 19+ centuries the separation of Christianity and Judaism takes place, followed by the future reunion of the two when Yeshua returns. The Seal has also become known as the "grafted in" emblem now being worn by many Jewish and gentile believers who know that the gentiles have been "grafted in" (Romans 11) to the Hebraic roots of the faith.

The Seal shows that Christianity (the fish) is connected through Hebraic roots (the star of David which points to Yeshua) and then to the Jewish people (the Menorah). The Seal pictures the unity that was present in this early stage of Christianity, in which Yeshua is the bond bringing the Christians and Jews together. In the next few chapters the unfortunate story of how this bond was broken will be reviewed. The Synagogue and Seal will be discussed further in Chapter 8, where the coming reunion of Christianity and Judaism is discussed.

Yahweh is revealing His plan for restoring the unity that had first existed in biblical Christianity. Paul describes this unity in Ephesians Chapter 2 as "the one new man", where Yeshua calls for the breaking down of "the middle wall of separation" between the Jews and the gentiles. Further, it will also be shown that Ephesians 2 and Ezekiel 37 are biblical accounts of the same reunion that will occur in the future. When Yeshua returns and establishes His Millennial Kingdom, the unity between Christians and Jews will once again be restored.

THE SAD STORY OF THE SEPARATION

The story of separation will refer to the following timeline of important historic events:

30 AD   Crucifixion and resurrection of Yeshua

46-58   Paul's missionary journeys

66-70   First Jewish revolt against Roman rule

70   Destruction of Jerusalem & 2nd temple; temple worship and sacrifice system ceased; start of separation between Jewish Christians and traditional Jews

70-115   Increasing disconnection of Christianity from Hebrew roots

132-135	2nd Jewish revolt against Roman rule; additional-wedge between Jewish Christians & Jews

132-135   2nd Jewish revolt against Roman rule; additional-wedge between Jewish Christians & Jews

135-136   Destruction of Jerusalem—Jews banned from city—gentiles take over church; leadership moves to Rome, Antioch, and Alexandria

185-254   Origen and other "fathers" promote allegorical interpretation of Scriptures, De-Judaizing Christianity

306   Constantine becomes 1st Christian Roman Emperor

312   He makes Christianity "official" religion of Roman Empire—he distributed funds to "certain ministers of the lawful and most holy catholic religion"— Roman Catholicism takes over and the church of Yeshua became the church of Constantine.

321   Sunday is "officially" substituted for Saturday as the day of Christian worship

325   At Council of Nicea, Easter is "officially" substituted for Passover and Constantine ". . . commands with all authority of the Emperor that whatever the bishops decide is the will of God"

330   By this time, Catholic church is in political power and is taking an increasing unbiblical stance toward the Jews. The church has moved from a Hebrew to a Greek world view. Persecution of Jews continues.

380   Catholic Christianity had become the established religion of the Roman empire.

160 – 430   Period during which Church "fathers" make numerous anti-Semitic statements: Irenaeus, Bishop of Lyon,177; Gregory, Bishop of Nyssa, 394;

Chrysostom, Bishop of Constantinople, 400; and others

480   Fall of Roman Empire

Note that during the first Jewish revolt in 66-70 AD against Roman rule, the Jewish Christians refused to fight alongside the traditional Jews, but instead fled to Pella in present-day Jordan. With the destruction of Jerusalem and the second temple in 70 AD, the separation between the Jewish Christians and the traditional Jews (Judaism) started. As Christianity started spreading northward and westward in the 100-130 period, the church was becoming more and more gentile. The destruction of Jerusalem a second time during the war against Roman rule during 132-135, with the Jewish Christians again refusing to fight, continued the separation. The Jews by now had been scattered to many other countries, fulfilling Yahweh's prophecy in Deuteronomy 28:64, where it is written:

> 64"Then the LORD will scatter you among all peoples, from one end of the earth to the other, and there you shall serve other gods, which neither you nor your fathers have known—wood and stone.

The destructions of Jerusalem in 70 AD and 135 AD and the consequent scattering of the Jewish people were taken as evidence by the gentile Christians that the Jews were no longer the chosen people. These destructions were thought to be appropriate punishment for the Jews because they crucified Yeshua. Early in the 2nd century we also see anti-Semitism beginning to appear in the writings of the church "fathers".

Here is how Professor Marvin Wilson has summarized the situation: "By the middle of the 2nd century the writings of the Church Fathers reveal considerable antagonism between gentile Christians and Jews . . . The posture of the Church was decisively set *against* the Synagogue. Whereas one gentile nation after another had responded positively to the Christian missionary outreach, the Synagogue continued to cling stubbornly to its ancestral faith, leaving the Church increasingly frustrated and embittered. Sermons, dialogues, diatribes, and polemics became the order of the day. The Church sought to conquer its opponent by demonstrating with every possible evidence that Judaism was a dead and legalistic faith. Thereby the schism became greater as Jews increasingly became victims of discrimination and contempt at the hands of those whose faith was said to have superseded theirs." *(1)*

Gentiles had essentially taken control of the church, and leadership had moved from Jerusalem to Rome, Alexandria, and Antioch. Replacement theology, wherein the church has replaced Israel, started emerging as a Christian doctrine. As Christianity continued its spread northward and westward, it started being modified and adjusted to "better fit" with the cultures of these regions. This aspect will be more fully explored in the next chapter when the effects of the religion Mithraism are discussed. For now, suffice it to say that the "better fit" came about through the blending of paganism with biblical Christianity.

By around 185, the church had spread into Europe, and westernization was bringing about significant variations to the Gospel that Jesus had taught. Christianity had severed its Hebraic roots – the child had disinherited its mother. Judaism remained firm in its stance that Yeshua was not the Messiah of Israel, while the Christian church had defined itself as a replacement of Judaism.

THE NAZARENE SECT – BIBLICAL CHRISTIANITY

Let us pause here before continuing and recall that *biblical* Christianity was, in fact, the Nazarene sect of Judaism. The Nazarenes were the early Christians and Yeshua was the sect's leader. In Matthew 2:23 it is written: 23And he came and dwelt in a city called Nazareth, that it might be fulfilled which was spoken by the prophets, "He shall be called a Nazarene."

And in Acts 24:5 it is also written about Paul: 5For we have found this man a plague, a creator of dissension among all the Jews throughout the world, and a ringleader of the sect of the Nazarenes.

Thus, Yeshua was the leader of the sect during His ministry, and then Paul became the "ring leader" around 60 AD. The Bible contains no additional information about the Nazarenes.

In 1999 the author visited Israel and attempted to find out what happened to the Nazarenes during the 2nd and 3rd centuries, as the church concurrently was being westernized and removed from its Hebraic roots. An interview with Professor Ray Pritz *(2)*, who is a scholar on early Jewish Christianity, provided the following information (all of which was subsequently confirmed by additional sources).

The Nazarenes, as might be expected, had rejected the church's setting aside the Hebrew Scriptures, which was Yeshua's Bible. They continued to observe them, which caused the eventual banishment of the Nazarenes from the church. They wanted to retain their dual identity – to both worship Yeshua and remain Jewish. As the church became increasingly gentile, the Nazarenes slowly faded away to isolated and fragmentary groups. So, we unfortunately see Yeshua's biblical Christianity being squeezed out of the picture.

There is some historical record of a Nazarene group in Persia in the 7th century, a group in a Jordan city, and groups in several other cities. But, by and large, the sect dwindled away, and the Jewish believers had no recourse but to be assimilated by the gentile Christian church. Fortunately, although the historical record of the Nazarenes is incomplete, Professor Pritz and other colleagues are working on a new book that will document, to the extent possible, the history of the sect. We know that groups of people continued to follow biblical Christianity because Yahweh has always had a "remnant" of believers throughout the generations, no matter how difficult the situation.

THE "CHURCH FATHERS" LEAD CHRISTIANITY AWAY FROM ITS HEBREW ROOTS

During the early centuries the "church fathers" continued the process of rejecting the Hebrew Scriptures by making vicious and hateful statements against the Jews. Following are some examples of what was being written and said:

• Justin Martyr stated that Jews are separated from other

nations and "justly suffer" because they have slain the Just One, and His prophets before Him, and now reject those who hope in Him.

- In the 3rd century Origen wrote: "And these calamities they (the Jews) have suffered because they were a most wicked nation, which, although guilty of many other sins, yet has been punished so severely for none, as those that were committed against our Jesus."(3)

- Around 380 Ambrose, bishop of Milan, praised the burning of a synagogue as an act pleasing to God.

- In the 4th century John Chrysostom, bishop of Antioch (called the golden-mouthed), spoke in particularly terrible language, as this sample shows: "Many, I know, respect the Jews and think that their present way of life is a venerable one. This is why I hasten to uproot and tear out this deadly opinion . . . the synagogue is not only a brothel and a theater; it is also a den of robbers and a lodging for wild beasts . . . when God forsakes a people, what hope of salvation is left? When God forsakes a place, that place becomes the dwelling of demons . . . The Jews live for their bellies, they gape for the things of this world, their condition is no better than that of pigs or goats because of their wanton ways and excessive gluttony. They know but one thing: to fill their bellies and be drunk." (4)

Here is how Dr. Richard Booker has described this era:

". . . teaching of grace without accountability . . . is a false teaching that developed early in the Christian era by the leading *'Church Fathers'. Many of them were Greek philosophers* (emphasis added). They despised the Jews, had no connection to the Hebraic background of the New Testament, and actively sought to sever Christianity from its Hebraic/Jewish roots. . . One very important individual who lived during the 2nd century was named Marcion. Marcion was a heretic who taught that the God of the Hebrew Scriptures (Old Testament) was a cruel God different from the God revealed in the New Testament. Marcion rejected the Hebrew Scriptures. . . his teachings contrasting law and grace heavily influenced many church leaders. Augustine was a great scholar who wrote a monumental work in the 5th century called *The City of God*. He promoted Marcion's idea contrasting law and grace as opposites. Augustine's writings influenced the church for centuries and unfortunately many of them were carried forward by the reformers at the time of the Protestant Reformation. *Marcion's false teachings on law and grace would become the core doctrine of much of Western Christianity that is taught today* (emphasis added). Unfortunately, the results of interpreting Hebraic concepts with a Greek mind have been disastrous for both Christianity and Judaism." (5)

This "disaster" will be more fully explored in Chapter 4, where it will be shown in considerable detail that "law" in our English Bibles is a complete mistranslation of what it really means. It should be further noted here that Augustine, the "father" of the early Catholic Church, authored many false teachings that are still haunting Christianity today. John Kennedy provides interesting perspective about him:

"In few places can we find the life of Catholic Christianity more aptly epitomized than in the life of Augustine. In Augustine we see the confusion of spiritual life and ideals with ecclesiastical barbarism . . . probably no man has made such a great contribution to the establishment of the Roman Church and the perpetuation of centuries of ruthlessness in the name of Christ. . . . Augustine lent his authority to traditionalism and sacramentalism, fostered belief in purgatory, and encouraged the use of relics which, in the hands of unscrupulous priests, was to become such a disgraceful and lucrative trade, playing upon the incredulity of superstitious people to fill the coffers of Catholicism and the pockets of her prelates." (6)

Marcion was also a chief contributor to the destruction of the church's Hebraic roots. Dr Charles Bryant-Abraham provides further insight on the damage created by his false teachings:

"Marcion was the son of the Greek Bishop of Sinope in the 2nd century AD. He became a ship-owner, a man of considerable wealth, and the leader of a powerful school of thought in early Proto-Catholicism, of which the influence in subtle ways endures to this day. Marcionism's most insidious tenet was the argument that there were two gods: one, the creator and judge, was a harsh Old Testament God ruling through fear and demanding obedience; the other, a god of spirit, light, and love, revealed by his son, Jesus – two entirely different gods. Marcion considered the Jewish Scriptures, which at that time were the only Christian Scriptures, as proceeding from the inferior creator-god. He therefore renounced and rejected them. . . Marcion's antagonism against the Torah and the Jewish people has overwhelmingly dominated Christian thought until today. . . . " (7)

The above statements of early "church fathers" were representative of the diatribes and lies often leveled at the Jews. They were men hard at work to completely separate Christianity from its Hebrew roots, and they were, unfortunately, very successful in their endeavors to do so. It's interesting that *The Essential Catholic Handbook* lists "Saint Ambrose, Saint Augustine, and Saint Chrysostom" as "fathers of the Church who had a major impact on the doctrinal development of the Church." At the same time, they caused a major increase in anti-Semitism.

CONSTANTINE, THE MITHRAIC CHRISTIAN

When Constantine came into power early in the 4th century, the church was transformed from the "persecutee" to the "persecutor" (of Judaism). His attachment to Mithraism will be covered later in this chapter and the next. The tables were seemingly turned, and Christianity looked to be on the road to victory. But there were some stumbling blocks that would prove to be massive.

Jesse Hurlbut explains it this way in his book on church history:

"In the year 305 when Diocletian (Roman Emperor) abdicated the imperial throne, the Christian religion was sternly prohibited, its profession was punished with torture and death, and against it all the power of the state was called into exercise. Less than eighty years afterward, in 380, Christianity was recognized as the official religion of the Roman Empire, and a Christian emperor held supreme authority with a court of professed Christians around them. *It seemed but a single step from facing lions in the amphitheatre to a place beside the throne of the world!* (emphasis added) . . . But while the triumph of Christianity resulted in much that was good, inevitably the alliance of the state and the church brought in its train many evils. The ceasing of persecution was a blessing, but the establishment of Christianity as the state religion became a curse. Everybody sought membership in the church, and nearly everybody was received. Both good and bad, sincere seekers after God and hypocritical seekers after gain, rushed into communion. Ambitious, worldly, unscrupulous men sought office in the church for social and political influence. The moral tone of Christianity in power was far below that which had marked the same people under persecution. The services of worship increased in splendor, but were less spiritual and hearty than those of former times. The forms and ceremonies of pagan gradually crept into the worship. Some of the old heathen feasts became church festivals with change of name and of worship." *(8)*

In 306 Constantine became the first Christian Roman Emperor. In 312 he made Christianity the official religion of the Roman Empire; in 321 Sunday is substituted for the Sabbath as the day of Christian worship; and then the crowning blow came in 325 when, by political decision, Easter is substituted for Passover at the Council of Nicea. These are the dates when the events became "official", but the substitutions had started much earlier.

It is of interest to see what happened at this Council, and Constantine's letters to the churches, contained in *Eusebius' Ecclesiastical History*, are very revealing. We can be rest assured of the validity of Eusebius' historical accounts because he was a life-long friend and admirer of Constantine, and in many ways his biographer. Justo Gonzalez in his book on Christian history had this to say about Eusebius: "Eusebius of Caesarea was in all probability the most learned Christian of his time. He was also one of the most ardent admirers of Constantine and his work, as may be seen in his quoted words: ' Looking westward or eastward, looking over the whole earth, and even looking at heaven, always and everywhere I see blessed Constantine leading the same Empire.'" *(9)*

Here are some of the provocative things Constantine had to say in one of his letters contained in *Eusebius' Ecclesiastical History:*

"Constantine, August, to the Churches: . . . I thought it especially incumbent on me to endeavor that the happy multitudes of the Catholic Church should preserve one faith, be united in unfeigned love, and harmoniously join in their devotions to Almighty God . . ."

(Constantine goes on and discusses decisions made at the Council meeting) . . .

"When the question arose concerning the most holy day of Easter, it was decreed by common consent to be expedient, that this festival should be celebrated on the same day by all, in every place . . . it seemed to everyone a most unworthy thing that we should follow the custom of the Jews in the celebration of this most holy solemnity, who, polluted wretches! having stained their hands with a nefarious crime, are justly blinded in their minds. It is fit, therefore, that rejecting the practice of this people, we should perpetuate to all future ages the celebration of this rite in a more legitimate order, which we have kept from the first day of our Lord's passion event to the present times. Let us then have nothing in common with the most hostile rabble of the Jews. . . A more lawful and proper course is open to our most holy religion. In pursuing this course with a unanimous consent, let us withdraw ourselves, my much honored brethren, from that most odious fellowship. . .

And, to sum up the whole in a few words, it was agreeable to the common judgment of all, that the most holy feast of Easter should be celebrated . . . This being the case, receive with cheerfulness the heavenly and truly divine command. *For whatever is transacted in the holy councils of the bishops, is to be referred to the divine will* . . .(emphasis added)

May God preserve you, my beloved brethren." (Signed by Constantine) *(10)*

The above demonstrates conclusively what the church "fathers" thought of the Jews – an example of terrible anti-Semitism. It also demonstrates how the traditions of men blatantly imposed themselves on the Word of Yahweh. Not only is a political decision made at the Council of Nicea to substitute the pagan rite Easter for Passover, but the *bishops are given authority to determine divine will.*

A few early fathers continued to observe the biblical time of Passover on 14 Nisan. Eusebius reported in his history that Polycarp, Bishop of Smyrna; Thraseas, Bishop of Eumenia; and Sagaris, Bishop of Laodicea all observed Passover on Nisan 14. He further stated that Polycarp "had always observed it with John the disciple of our Lord, and the rest of the apostles, with whom he associated."*(11)* These fathers had dissented from the majority who had voted for the substitution of Easter for Passover.

Historian John Kennedy said this about the Council: "The result of the Council was the formulation of a statement of doctrine . . . which concluded with the anathemas of the 'holy Catholic and apostolic Church' upon those who did not consent to it . . . Nicea was a culmination of the inevitable movement towards centralization in the ecumenical Church's authority." *(12)*

Constantine maintained his worship of a sun god all through his "Christian" experience. Justo Gonzalez provides additional insight concerning his sun worship:

"His own father had been a devotee of the Unconquered Sun. . . . During most of his political career, Constantine seems to have thought that the Unconquered Sun and the Christian God were compatible – perhaps two views of the same supreme deity — and that the other gods, although subordinate, were nevertheless real and relatively powerful. . . . if he had attempted to suppress pagan worship, he would have had to face an irresistible opposition. The ancient gods were far from forgotten. Christianity had made very little progress among the old aristocracy and the rural masses. There were in the army many followers of *Mithra and other gods* (emphasis added). The Academy of Athens and the Museum of Alexandria, the two great learning centers of the time, were devoted to the study of ancient pagan wisdom. . . . The official religion of the Empire was Paganism, and as head of that Empire Constantine took the title of Supreme Pontiff or High priest. . . In 324 an imperial edict ordered all soldiers to worship the Supreme God on the first day of the week (Sunday) . . . it was also the day of the Unconquered Sun, and therefore the pagans saw no need to oppose such an edict." *(13)*

The Unconquered Sun and Yahweh compatible? Many followers of Mithra? Great learning centers studying pagan wisdom? No wonder biblical Christianity was led off track early in its existence.

The institution of the early Catholic Church was born and grew in formidable power during these centuries, modifying *biblical* Christianity in the process. *It is not the purpose here to denounce or vilify Catholicism*; however, the truth of what happened early in the life of Christianity simply cannot be covered up. Early Roman Catholicism *did take over and significantly change the biblical* Christianity established by Yeshua and the apostles. The historical facts showing this are indisputable, and it would be a complete distortion and a continuation of the cover-up to state the situation otherwise.

John Kennedy summarized it this way: "Christianity became fashionable. Although Constantine himself was not a committed Christian, he encouraged others to accept the faith, and there were plenty of people ready to accept anything if, in doing so, they earned the commendation of the State. There was therefore, a great influx of pagans into the Christian Church, pagans who had been Christianized by learning the rudiments of the faith, but who, nevertheless, were still pagans at heart. . . the State was accorded a recognized say in Church matters . . . the development of a hierarchial form of government within the Church inevitably brought with it a sense of quasi-political rivalry and a lust for power . . . the *degeneration of the Church had set the stage for the unholy alliance between Church and State.*" (emphasis added) *(14)*

Dr. John Garr also has written an informative capsule summary of Constantine's part in the severing of Christianity from its Hebraic roots: "Christianity was systematically excised from its Jewish roots, as one by one the church transplanted the teachings of Jesus in the foreign soil of human tradition. The final blow of the Greco-Roman axe which severed Christianity from the tap root of Judaism was wielded by Constantine the Great, *pontifex maximus* of Roman polytheism, when he arrogated to himself the headship of the church, enjoined the observance of Sunday as a day of worship in the Roman Empire, and outlawed any practice in the church which was obviously rooted in Judaism."*(15)*

Dave Hunt has also described Constantine's pagan baggage:

"The very idea of a Church Council was invented by Constantine, who, in spite of his professed 'conversion' to Christ, remained a pagan. He never renounced his loyalty to the many pagan gods. . . the sun god, not Christ, continued to be honored on the imperial coins." *(16)*

THE FISCUS JUDAICUS

Before moving to the next chapter, another event took place in the first century which is of interest and pertinent to the separation. The Romans had decided after the 66-70 AD war with the Jews to punish them by exacting a special tax known as the Fiscus Judaicus (Jewish Tax), which amounted to two day's wages per person per year *(17)*. This was just one more factor contributing to the separation of the Christian church from Judaism.

O'Quin points out that: "The impact this tax would have on the development of the early church was significant for it struck at the heart of Jewish/Christian identity. If the tax were to be levied against all Jews, the question had to be asked, 'who is a Jew?' . . . An important consequence of the tax was that it forced the various communities to define themselves as either Jewish or non-Jewish." *(17)*

Thus, gentile believers who wanted to avoid the tax had to demonstrate that they were not part of "Jewish Christianity". They somehow had to show that they had not adopted the Jewish way of life. They accomplished this by adopting traditions that could be explained as non-Jewish, and O'Quin shows their success in this: "So we see that by 110 AD the Roman government was able to look upon the Christian community as separate and distinct from the Synagogue. . . . From a Roman perspective, the Christian Church had found a way to redefine its faith so as to be seen wholly independent from that of the Jewish communities."

The main way the church used to show this "independence" was to significantly downplay the Torah. After 96 AD the early church fathers set aside Torah references almost entirely in their numerous writings, while prior to this date they had relied almost totally on them. Thus, as O'Quin summarizes: "At the very same time Rome was discouraging Torah observance through taxation, the gentilized church was developing a theology of disassociation with Torah and all things Jewish."

We will see in Chapter 4 how harmful it was for the church to disassociate itself from the Hebrew Scriptures/Torah. The very foundation for the New Testament was eaten away as the church distanced itself from the Torah. It is difficult to quantify the impact of the Judaicus tax on the separation process, but it definitely was significant in causing 2nd century Christianity to redefine itself in other than Jewish terms.

In summary, history shows clearly how Christianity, as it moved from Israel into other countries, gradually was taken over by the gentiles. As the church became predominantly gentile, Yeshua's Nazarene sect, true *biblical* Christianity, dwindled away to obscurity. The early "church fathers", who were seeking their own brand of Christianity, led the church away from Yahweh's and Yeshua's intended path.

The historical evidence is overwhelming: Anti-Semitism became more pronounced than ever in the early centuries, so much so that the early "church fathers" became blinded to Bible truth. They simply disregarded Scripture in their lies and blasphemies concerning the Jews – their attitude toward them can only be described as completely *anti-Christian*. The extent of the damage cannot even be completely assessed. Certainly *biblical* Christianity was severely compromised, because Chapter 4 will show that this vicious anti-Semitism caused the church to, in effect, throw away Yahweh's intended spiritual applications in His Hebrew Scriptures/Torah.

Think about it – a group of men during the 2nd through the 5th centuries subverted the very Word of God – they were able to turn it into their own religion.

Only a few of numerous historical resources have been used to document the above sad story. How and why this separation took place is probably one of the best-documented issues in history. There is no question that biblical Christianity was turned into the Holy Roman Catholic Church, which will be clearly shown in the next chapter.

Exodus 23:13: "And in all that I have said to you, be circumspect and *make no mention of the name of other gods, nor let it be heard from your mouth.*

Matthew 15:3: He answered and said to them, "Why do you also transgress the commandment of God because of your tradition?"

Mark 7:8: For laying aside the commandment of God, you hold the tradition of men.

How odd of God to choose the Jew,
But not so odd as those who choose
The Jewish God and hate the Jew. (Author unknown)

3. THE RELIGION MITHRAISM and ANTI-SEMITISM

<hr>

"Mithras, God of the Morning, our trumpets waken the Wall!
Rome is above the Nations, but Thou art over all!"
(Rudyard Kipling, *A Song to Mithras*)

HOW PAGANISM BECAME PART OF CHRISTIANITY

In the previous chapter, we saw how the separation between the Christian church and Judaism occurred during the early centuries after Yeshua and His disciples were gone. This chapter shows that the early "church fathers" used many of the pagan rites coming out of Mithraism in moving biblical Christianity away from the path that Yeshua had carefully established. They created their own "part pagan/part biblical" religion.

Mithraism focused on sun worship, and Mithras was the religion's sun god. The worship of the sun was known as *Mithras Solis Invictus,* which means "Mithras, the unconquered sun". *(1)* Recall from the previous chapter that Constantine and his father worshipped the unconquered sun. Sun-day was the day for honoring Mithras, and December 25th was observed as his birthday. Chapter 6 will show that the Bible points to the time of the Feast of Tabernacles as being approximately the time of Yeshua's birth. This is an example of blending paganism with biblical Christianity –

celebrating Yeshua's birth on the birthday of the pagan sun god, Mithras. What an insult to Almighty Yahweh!

The Roman Emperors were instrumental in supporting sun worship, and it can be seen that Constantine also was under its spell. In his confusion about Mithras and Yeshua, he blended them together, bringing the pagan background of sun-worship into biblical Christianity (hence "Sun-day" instead of the 7th day Sabbath).

Mithraism can actually be traced as far back as Nimrod, who in Genesis started a false religion to compete with Yahweh. Off and on through the centuries since then, Babylon has been competing with biblical belief to gain the hearts and minds of people. Babylon's false worship is still present today in different forms all over the world. It appeared in ancient Persia and Syria in the form of Mithraism, and then spread into the Roman Empire, where it became the main religion of the Emperors and the Roman army. Mithraic doctrine, as will be shown, has many similarities with biblical doctrine, making it possible to mislead people into following false religious precepts.

An unknown historian once said, "The entire European continent and the New World would be Mithraic today if Christianity hadn't come along". Other historians have put it another way: "Christianity didn't conquer Mithraic Paganism. Mithraism blended in and changed names." *(1)* The previous chapter showed the prime example of a name change: the name "Passover" was changed to "Easter" by a political stroke of the pen at the Council of Nicea in 325. Other name changes will be discussed in subsequent chapters.

NUMEROUS AUTHORS HAVE
WRITTEN ABOUT MITHRAISM

Some of the many historical resources discussing Mithraism are quoted below in order to illustrate the broad range of them. These sources include encyclopedias, historians, reference books, and others. It is remarkable that Mithraism is unknown to most Christians, given the numerous times it has been written about. Has the church been hiding this religion for fear that its pagan connections to Sunday and the date December 25th are so apparent? Why are not seminaries including the study of Mithraism in their curricula?

"Originally an Aryan god, Mithras was worshipped in Iran as the god of contracts. He preserves truth and order, destroying the disruptive forces of evil, anger, greed, pride and procrastination . . . . Mithras is an important and popular deity in Iranian (Persian) history. . . He still occupies an important place in Zoroastrian ritual. . . Mithraism first entered Rome in 60 BC, and in the second century AD it spread through the empire as far as Britain. . . . The central belief of the cult was the sacrifice of a bull by Mithras. This act was both creative and redemptive. The worshipper looked back to a sacrifice at the beginning, when life had come out of death, and forward to the final sacrifice by Mithras when the last animal to die would give men the elixir of immortality. *A foretaste of this divine gift could be shared in the regular communion meal of bread and wine in which the priest represented Mithras.*"(emphasis added) *(2)*

"Mithraism was the largest pagan religion in the Roman and Greek world at the time of its rival religion, Christianity. The Mithraists were keeping the winter festival called 'nativity of the sun', thus named because they believed that the sun was born each year on December 25. They also celebrated December 25 as the date of Mithras' birthday because he was their sun god. The religious headquarters of Mithraism was at Rome."*(3)*

"The immense popularity of this cult should not be underestimated. The monuments dedicated to this system are scattered all over the Roman Empire and right through Europe. . . . The conflict between Mithraism and Christianity was so great that for a time the outcome hung in the balance. The fact of the matter is that the result was decided by adopting their practices and giving them Christian names." *(4)*

"It is one of the great ironies of history that Romans ended up worshipping the god of their chief political enemy, the Persians. The Roman historian Quintas Rufus recorded in his book *History of Alexander* that before going into battle against the anti-Mithraic country of Rome, the Persian soldiers would pray to Mithras for victory. However, after the two enemy civilizations had been in contact for more than a thousand years, the worship of Mithras finally spread to the Romans. The Romans viewed Persia as a land of wisdom and mystery, and Persian religious teachings appealed to those Romans who found the established state religion uninspiring. . . . At a time when Christianity was only one of several dozen foreign Eastern cults struggling for recognition in Rome, the religious dualism and dogmatic moral teaching of Mithraism set it apart from the other sects, creating a stability previously unknown in Roman paganism. Early Roman worshippers imagined themselves to be keepers of ancient wisdom from the far east, and invincible heroes of the faith, ceaselessly fighting the powers of corruption. Mithrasim quickly gained prominence and remained the most important pagan religion until the end of the 4th century. . . In Rome, more than a hundred inscriptions dedicated to Mithras have been found, in addition to 75 sculpture fragments, and a series of Mithraic temples situated in all parts of the city. One of the largest Mithraic temples built in Italy now lies under the present site of the Church of St. Clemente, near the Colosseum in Rome." *(5)*

"After the peace of the Church of Rome, to facilitate the acceptance of the faith by the pagan masses, (Rome) found it convenient to institute the 25th of December as the feast of the temporal birth of Christ, to divert them from the pagan feast, celebrated on the same day in honour of the "Invincible Sun" Mithras, the conqueror of darkness. *(6)*

"Christianity stepped into an open climate, religiously. In a sort of 'new age' movement many people had begun to embrace eastern religions – the worship of Isis, Dionysus, Mithras, Cybele, and others. Worshipers searched for new beliefs." *(7)*

"The Persians spread the worship of Mithra, called Mithraism, throughout Asia Minor. The cult became popular, especially among Roman soldiers and slaves. By about 100 AD, they had spread it into Europe. Mithraism ranked as a principal competing religion of Chrstianity until the 300's." *(8)*

"Catholicism has preserved some of the outer forms of Mithraism; to name some, the timing of Christmas . . . Christian priests becoming 'Father' despite Jesus' specific proscription of the acceptance of such title. The Mithraic Holy Father wore a red cap and garment and a ring, and carried a shepherd's staff. The Head

Christian adopted the same title and outfitted himself in the same manner." *(9)*

Mithraism included some ritual services that sound familiar: the eucharist (a form of communion), the rosary, sacrifice of the mass, prayers for the dead, and others. The leader of the services was titled "Pater", and he had five levels of hierarchy in his organization. It seems rather apparent that this was the early foundation for the Roman Catholic Church.

The Catholic Encyclopedia expends considerable time and space trying to distance Catholicism from Mithraism. At one point it states: "Some apparent similarities exist; but in a number of details it is quite probable that Mithraism was the borrower from (Catholic) Christianity."

Given the historical record of Mithraism, which is much more ancient, Catholicism obviously came into existence later. It is not logical that "Mithraism was the *borrower* from (Catholic) Christianity". However, even if the Catholic Encyclopedia has it reversed, it is really admitting that both religions are similar. Regardless of whom borrowed from whom, the net result is the same – *Catholicism is very similar to Mithraism.*

The latter half of the following summary shows the similarities common to both:

o Mithraism was prominent during the 0-300 AD period and was the primary competitor of Christianity.

o Mithraism centered on sun-worship. "Mithras" was the religion's sun-god.

o Mithraism was allied with Zoroastrianism, which originated in ancient Persia.

o Sun-worship was increasingly emphasized by Roman emperors during 0-300 AD. "Sun-day" was the day for honoring Mithras.

o December 25 was observed as Mithras' birthday.

o Mithraism included a Eucharist, the rosary, sacrifice of the mass, prayers for the dead, and justification by works in its worship.

o Baptism was necessary for salvation.

o The leader of ritual services was titled "pater", and over the "paters" was the "High Pater".

o There were five levels of hierarchy within the Mithraism religion.

THE RESULT OF BLENDING THE ABOVE PAGAN DOCTRINE WITH BIBLICAL CHRISTIANITY PRODUCED CATHOLICISM

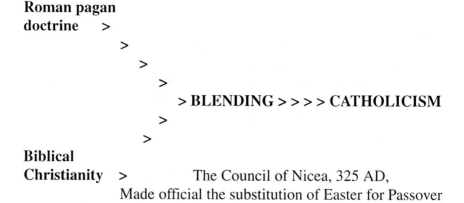

Roman pagan doctrine >

      >

        >

          >

            > BLENDING > > > > CATHOLICISM

        >

      >

Biblical Christianity >   The Council of Nicea, 325 AD, Made official the substitution of Easter for Passover

As difficult as it is to accept the idea that biblical Christianity was compromised in significant ways, history documents that this is the case. Even if we did not have the benefit of knowing about the history of Mithraism, we should still be very suspicious of the fact that Sunday was "officially" substituted for the Sabbath, and Easter for Passover, by the Holy Roman Empire early in the 4th century without any Scriptural justification for doing so. Again, this "official" recognition of Sun-day and Easter took place after several centuries of integrating Sun-day and Easter into the Christian worship pattern.

However, even though early Roman Catholicism had taken over

Christianity, history shows that there still were pockets of *biblical* Christianity that stayed true to Yeshua's Bible. The Nazarene Sect discussed in Chapter 2 was certainly a prime example. These groups of biblical Christians, and likely many isolated individuals, rejected the early Catholic Church and worshiped according to the Bible.

The fact that the Bible mentions "Sabbath" over 160 times, and Sunday not once, provides a strong indication that something is wrong. Yeshua never changed the Sabbath to Sunday- -man did. He and His followers honored it throughout the New Testament as the 7th day of the week, while Sunday is clearly the 1st day of the week. The New Testament contains numerous passages showing how Yeshua and the disciples were so faithful in keeping the Sabbath and the other Leviticus 23 appointments. These instances will be covered in later chapters.

Thus, the blending of Roman pagan doctrine, Mithraism, with *biblical* Christianity further increased disconnection from its Hebrew roots. Numerous authors have carefully documented how and why Mithraism became part of the church. The combination of certain early "church fathers" and Mithraism caused the church to reject spiritual input from the Torah, adding more fuel to the fire of separation. The Protestant Reformation in the 1500s only went part way in ridding Christianity of the unbiblical practices relating to early Catholicism, because it did not also cause a return to the Hebrew Scriptures/Torah and important biblical practices; such as, observing the Sabbath and keeping Yahweh's Leviticus 23 appointments.

ANTI-SEMITISM: RETURNING IN A BIG WAY

The anti-Semitism of Martin Luther, who led the Protestant Reformation, was not mentioned in Chapter 2, but it should be discussed here. Luther initially was very positive toward the Jews, and in the early 1500s he authored a tract entitled, *That Jesus Christ Was Born a Jew*. However, when they resisted his attempts to convert them to Christianity, he completely turned against them. Marvin Wilson describes it in this way: "When he (Luther) saw that the Jews failed to respond to the Christian message, he became hostile toward them. He issued a series of vitriolic statements, including *On the Jews and Their Lies* (1543). In these bitter diatribes he labeled Jews as "venomous", "thieves", and "disgusting vermin". Furthermore, Luther called for Jews to be permanently driven out of the country." *(10)*

Luther had become an anti-Semite on a par with the other "church fathers" discussed in Chapter 2. Several centuries later the Nazis would rise to power in Germany, and based largely on Luther's writings, they were motivated to try to exterminate the Jewish people through the Holocaust. They nearly succeeded, murdering about six million along the way.

Dave Hunt has provided an excellent description of the linkages among anti-Semitism, Catholicism, Luther, and the Nazis: "The Roman Catholic popes were the first to develop anti-Semitism to a science. Hitler, who remained a Catholic to the end, would claim that he was only following the example of both Catholics and Lutherans in finishing what the Church had begun. Anti-Semitism was a part of his Catholicism from which Martin Luther was never freed. He advocated burning down Jews' homes and giving them the choice between conversion and having their tongues torn out." *(11)*

Other attempts to destroy the Jews have been made over the centuries; for example, Haman in the book of Esther around 450 BC, Antiochus Epiphanes around 165 BC, Rome in 70 AD, the Russian pogroms around 1880-1925, and now the Arabs/Islam once again. Anti-Semitism is somehow ingrained in most of the world. Today, it is once again gaining momentum everywhere, mainly because the world's leading terrorist (and Nobel Peace Prize winner??), Yasser Arafat, has convinced just about every country, through deceptions and lies, that the Jews are the instigators of the Middle East problems. Numerous fire-bombings of synagogues have occurred recently throughout Europe, and many people are asking if this portends a return to pre-WWII conditions in Germany.

In an April syndicated column, George Will wrote: "Anti-Semitism is a stronger force in world affairs than it has been since it went into a remarkably brief eclipse after the liberation of the Nazi extermination camps in 1945. The United Nations, supposedly an embodiment of lessons learned from the war that ended in 1945, is now the instrument for lending spurious legitimacy to the anti-Semites' war against the Jewish state founded by the survivors of that war. . . Anti-Semitism is not directed against the behavior of the Jews but against the *existence* of the Jews."(emphasis added)

In a recent newsletter the president of Harvard University wrote as follows: "Consider some of the global events of the last year. There have been synagogue burnings, physical assaults on Jews, or the painting of swastikas on Jewish memorials in every country in Europe. Observers in many countries have pointed to the worst outbreak of attacks against Jews since the Second World War . . . The United Nations-sponsored World Conference on Racism – while failing to mention human rights abuses in China, Rwanda, or any place in the Arab world – spoke of Israel's policies prior to recent struggles under the Barak government as constituting ethnic cleansing and crimes against humanity." *(12)*

The *Protocols of the Elders of Zion*, which is a proven fictitious plan for Jewish domination of the world, was made public in the early part of the 20th Century. It was originally fabricated by the USSR, and was spread in the U.S. by Henry Ford, among others. It is now being serialized by the *Arab Voice* newspaper in Patterson, N.J. Arab and Muslim institutions are leading advocates of anti-Semitism in both the Middle East and the U.S.

John Garr has emphasized that during the Protestant Reformation in the 16th century anti-Semitism was not repudiated: "At the beginning of the sixteenth century, God started a restoration of the Christianity of the first century . . . one thing that was tragically overlooked in the reformation, however, was the spirit of anti-Semitism which its leaders failed to purge from their midst. The fathers of Protestantism simply failed to restore their reformed Christianity to its inherent Jewish ideals." *(13)*

Even American Airlines has recently exhibited the "curse" of anti-Semitism. Some frequent flyer correspondence from AA has renamed Israel as the "Held Territories". A national campaign against this policy has resulted in American's back-tracking and trying to trivialize this, but the initial intent is clearly anti-Semitic. *(14)* The truth is that Israel is presently occupying far less land than Yahweh gave them, and as Chapters 7 and 8 will show, *Israel will be restored to all of this land,* and probably much more before the end of this age.

Example after example are in the media showing that anti-Semitism is raising its ugly head in ways very much like the Hitler era, only now it is around the world. When the time is right, Yahweh will act to administer His justice to those engaged in the curse of anti-Semitism. Anti- Semitic nations in the past, including Germany and the USSR, have all gone by the wayside, as have individual anti-Semites. It's too bad that individuals and nations in the present day have not paid attention to what their ultimate fate will be based on what has happened in the past. Genesis 12:3 makes it abundantly clear that *those who curse Israel will be cursed by Yahweh.*

Ramon Bennett in his book, *Saga,* expressed it this way: "A good number of nations have been destroyed over the millennia due to their treatment of Israel and the Jewish people. We shall explore the biblical accounts of those nations and find the reason for their destruction – religious, political, social and moral sins. We find, too, a clear warning that any nation committing the same sin invites the same judgment." *(15)*

The mixing of biblical Christianity and Mithraism, combined with independent efforts by the "church fathers" to put their own spin on the Bible, produced a "partially pagan/partially biblical" church – the early Holy Roman Catholic Church. The result was separation and alienation between the Jews and Christians, which led the church into the intense anti-Semitism of the past and the increase of it that is occurring in the present day.

Exodus 23:13: "And in all that I have said to you, be circumspect and *make no mention of the name of other gods, nor let it be heard from your mouth.*

I Kings 11: [33] they have forsaken Me, and worshiped Ashtoreth the goddess of the Sidonians, Chemosh the god of the Moabites, and Milcom the god of the people of Ammon, and have not walked in My ways

Col 2: [8]Take heed lest there shall be any one that maketh spoil of you through his philosophy and vain deceit, after the tradition of men, after the rudiments of the world, and not after Christ:

Matthew 15:9 But in vain do they worship me, Teaching as their doctrines the precepts of men.

4. THE TRUTH ABOUT THE TORAH

Luke 6:46: **"But why do you call me 'Lord, Lord,' and not do the things which I say?"**

Jeremiah 16:10-11: what *is* our sin that we have committed against the LORD our God?' [11]then you shall say to them, 'Because your fathers have forsaken Me,' says the LORD; 'they have walked after other gods and have served them and worshiped them, and have forsaken Me and not kept My law *(Torah).*

Given the background of the previous chapters, it should not be difficult to understand that the potential for serious distortions of biblical Christianity existed. This chapter will focus on *one distortion* that has created immeasurable problems in the church's correct understanding of the Bible: *the mistranslation of "Torah" in the Hebrew Scriptures into "law" in our English Bibles.* This major mistranslation is at the root cause for the church's rejection of spiritually applying the Hebrew Scriptures/Torah, because the *teaching and instruction aspects of the Torah* became hidden in the *"law"* of our English Bibles. This will be discussed in considerable detail because of the great significance of the issue.

INTRODUCTION

An excellent way to introduce this topic is to quote Professor

Marvin Wilson's analysis of the early church fathers' thinking process, or lack thereof, concerning the **problem of what to do with the Old Testament.** Should they destroy it and complete once and for all the separation of the church from Judaism? Or, should they *allegorize and spiritualize it* (develop "new" meanings for Hebraic thoughts) in order to change it into a suitable "Christian" document? They **decided to go the allegory route:**

"The early Church Fathers had to solve the problem of what to do with the Old Testament. Their anti-Judaic stance forced them to view the Jewish Scriptures with its many strange laws and customs as offensive at worst and little more than antiquated at best. In addition, the position of the Church was that it had replaced Israel. No longer a remnant within Israel, it had become a separate gentile body. (The Church decided) to save the Old Testament from total destruction and . . . it found an **alternative solution – allegory**. In allegory, the Old Testament could be made a "Christian" document. Through their efforts to spiritualize, typologize, and christologize the text, the early Church Fathers were able to find abundant Christian meaning in the Old Testament. Christ, or New Testament thought, was read into, rather than out of, the biblical text in some of the most obscure places. Accordingly, Irenaeus, Origen, Augustine, and others developed a system of allegorical exegesis (system of interpretation), that had the disastrous effect of wrenching the biblical text from its plain historical meaning." *(1)* (emphasis added)

Most of this chapter addresses the Hebrew Scriptures (Old Testament) and the Torah, and the connections to the New Testament. Although the "Torah" is often defined to be the first five books of the Hebrew Scriptures, it also has the broader definition of referring to all of the Hebrew Scriptures. This broader definition is used here, and the term "Hebrew Scriptures/Torah" is frequently used to remind us of this.

The term "Torah-based lifestyle" is used several times in subsequent chapters. The perfect model of the Torah-based lifestyle is Yeshua Himself. One of the major doctrines of the New Testament is for believers to be like Him – to try and emulate what He does. To do this, we need to obey, as best we can, the same teachings and commandments that He obeyed, which are none other than the Hebrew Scriptures/Torah. He would have sinned had He not obeyed the Torah.

The New Covenant states clearly that, for both Jewish and non-Jewish believers, Yahweh will put His Torah "in their minds and write them on their hearts." (Jeremiah 31:31-34; Hebrews 8:7-12) The foundation, or beginning, of a Torah-based lifestyle is to observe the Sabbath and Yahweh's Leviticus 23 appointments, because doing so follows specific biblical teachings and commands that Yeshua obeyed. As believers grow spiritually, they can add to this foundation by striving to be obedient in other areas where Yeshua demonstrated His Torah-based lifestyle. The substitution of "Torah" for "law" in this discussion and in the referenced passages will be justified in what follows.

The forced separation of Christianity and Judaism by the early "Church fathers" and Mithraism caused the church to reject Yahweh's Torah, thereby leading it to depart from *true biblical* Christianity. By carefully reviewing critical passages in both Testaments, it can be conclusively shown that the Torah is a major part of the foundation for the *entire* Bible – not only the Hebrew Scriptures. Most often in our English Bibles the words "law" and "commandment" really mean "Torah". Yahweh and Yeshua will undoubtedly hold accountable the people, in earlier and later centuries, who taught against or neglected the Torah. Numerous passages show that the rejection of the Torah caused the very teachings of Yahweh to be cast aside. This is something worth thinking about, for as Yeshua clearly said in Matthew 5:19: "Whoever therefore breaks one of the least of these commandments (TORAH), and teaches men so, shall be called least in the kingdom of heaven; but whoever does and teaches them, shall be called great in the kingdom of heaven."

The repercussions of rejecting the Torah resound today. Foremost has been the accelerated growth of vicious anti-Semitism. Also, most Christians have been led away from knowing the *joy* of the Sabbath and Yahweh's holy appointments (Leviticus 23 feasts). For 19 centuries Christians have been taught that these are "Jewish things" that can be ignored.

The Sabbath and Yahweh's appointments have been replaced by

"Christian" holidays and events – nearly all of which are plainly based on pagan rites and traditions. Yahweh's calendar, which is so simple to understand, has also been replaced by a calendar that is based on Greek and Roman mythology. Months and days of the week are named after their deities, rather than the biblical names or numbers in the Bible. Rejection of the Torah by the church *is the root cause* for these departures from biblical Christianity.

Unfortunately, Christian scholars in the past have been blinded to the truth of the Torah. In his Foreword to the book, *They Loved the Torah*, Ariel Berkowitz said: "That over the centuries, many godly and sincere scholars have missed seeing the Torah faithfulness of Yeshua and his students (who later were the writers of Scripture themselves), is an amazing fact. They have asserted, instead, that Yeshua's atoning death and miraculous Resurrection rendered the Torah inoperative. Furthermore, they have taught that since Yeshua fulfilled the Torah, his followers (including us, today) have no responsibility to live it." *(2)*

This chapter will show that *only the "law part"* of the Torah is obsolete because Yeshua saved us from the "law of sin and death" (Romans 8:1-2). This is also affirmed by Romans 6:23 which states that "the wages of sin is death", but Yeshua gives us eternal life. He fulfilled every detail of the Torah to demonstrate for us the importance of Yahweh's teachings and instructions *beyond the "law part"*. We have the responsibility to do the best we can to follow His modeling of it.

Dr. Frederick Schweitzer offers the interesting comment that the Torah is the facilitator of Christian reunion, which is the subject of Chapter 8, but the comment also has relevance here: "That Judaism is the common denominator of all Christian bodies is an idea stated most memorably by Karl Barth in Church Dogmatics, where he writes that the 'Church must live with the Synagogue, not . . . (merely) as with another religion or denomination, but as with the root from which it has itself has sprung.' Barth once suggested that the most obvious facilitator of Christian reunion would be for the Christian churches to gain a more profound consciousness and enhanced knowledge of their Jewish origins." *(3)*

Since the Torah is the very heart and soul of Judaism, we see from his comment that the church needs to cultivate the Torah. Unfortunately, Christianity has by and large neglected the spiritual applications in the Hebrew Scriptures/Torah because of a complete misunderstanding of the word "law", which is frequently used in the New Testament. Usually, when a Christian sees "law", the immediate defensive thought is, "I am not under the law because Jesus saved me from it". Christians are taught this thought process by the church. Yes, Yeshua has saved us from the *law of sin and death*, because He died for our *sin* to save us from eternal *death*. Romans 8:1-2 clearly states this important truth: [1]*There is* therefore now no condemnation to those who are in Christ Jesus, who do not walk according to the flesh, but according to the Spirit. [2]For the law of the Spirit of life in *Christ Jesus has made me free from the law of sin and death.* (emphasis added)

However, while He saved us from "the law of sin and death" (the "law part" of the Torah), He still wants us to follow Yahweh's teachings and instructions in the Hebrew Scriptures/Torah to help us live in ways pleasing to Him. Because of translation problems, the "teachings and instructions" aspects, hidden in the "law" of our English Bibles, have been lost.

THE TORAH – YAHWEH'S TEACHINGS and INSTRUCTIONS and "LAW"

"Law" as most often used in English translations of the Hebrew Scriptures/Torah is Strong's word 8451 (see Glossary); however, "law" is "Torah" in the Hebrew. The root word of "Torah" is "yara", and taken together, "torah" and "yara" have the meanings "teach", "instruct", and "law". Torah's meaning also includes the idea of "shooting an arrow that hits the target." So, in the context of the original Hebrew Scriptures, the Hebrew word "Torah" represents Yahweh's teaching, instruction and law.

When the word "law" is used in our Bibles it most often is actually referring to the "Torah"(which extends to all of the Hebrew Scriptures). Torah includes the "law", but more importantly, it refers to the "teachings" and "instructions" of Yahweh. This is clear from the Bible; for example, Malachi 4:6 is the last time "law" (Torah) is mentioned in the Hebrew Scriptures, where Yahweh says

"Remember the law (Torah)".

Ariel and D'vorah Berkowitz have expressed it this way: "Hence, we can say that 'Torah' is God's teaching, hitting the mark of man's needs, including his need to know who God is and what His righteousness looks like. Torah is a document in which God has revealed Himself to mankind and taught us about Himself and His righteousness." *(4)*

TORAH IN THE HEBREW SCRIPTURES AND NEW TESTAMENT

Malachi 4:6 is the last time law (Torah) is used in the Hebrew Scriptures/Torah, and the first time it is used in the New Testament is Matthew 5:17. Matthew 5:17-19 states:

> Do not think that I came to destroy the Law (Torah) or the
> Prophets. I did not come to destroy
> But to fulfill. (18) For assuredly, I say to you, till heaven and
> earth pass away, one jot or one
> Tittle will by no means pass from the law (Torah) till all is
> fulfilled. (19) Whoever therefore
> Breaks one of the least of these commandments, and teaches
> men so, shall be called least in the
> Kingdom of heaven; but whoever does and teaches them, he
> shall be called great in the kingdom
> Of heaven.

Did Yahweh find that He had made a gross error in the 400 year interval between Malachi 4 and Matthew 5? Did He waffle and decide that the "Torah" of the Hebrew Scriptures should now be understood as just the "law" in the New Testament? The answer is obvious—He doesn't make mistakes, and He sent Yeshua to expand and teach the Torah. Yes, Yeshua *did save* us from the "law" of sin and death, when He was sacrificed on the tree/cross to cover our sin, but He obeyed and interpreted the Torah so that we would be able to follow His modeling of it. In John 14:15 Yeshua said, "if you love me, keep my commandments". His commandments are found in the Torah, His only Bible at the time, and He obeyed every "jot and tittle" of these commandments.

The remainder of Chapter 5, Chapter 6 and Chapter 7 contain a number of specific ways in which He explains, interprets, and expands the "law" (Torah). For example, in Matthew 5:21-22 He says "You heard that it was said . . . But I tell you that . . ." Similarly, in v. 33 He says "Again, you have heard that . . . but I tell you . . ." Chapters 5, 6 and 7 are really a "mini-Torah" which Yeshua is teaching. He is fully preaching the Torah so that we will be certain to understand it, and with His help we can then aspire to a Torah-based lifestyle. He is also correcting any faulty teaching that had been passed from generation to generation through extrabiblical material.

Verse 19 should be emphasized again. Yeshua is clearly saying how crucial it is to teach and follow the Torah. Teachers will be called "great in the kingdom of heaven" if they faithfully teach the Torah, but they will be "least" if they do not. This can only mean that when we enter the Millennium each of us will be placed somewhere within Yahweh's and Yeshua's "kingdom hierarchy", commensurate with how we treated the Torah. If we ignore it, we can count on being low in the hierarchy.

OTHER WAYS FOR SHOWING THAT "LAW" IS REALLY "TORAH"

When the Hebrew Scriptures were translated into Greek (the Septuagint) around 300 - 200 BC, the Greek word "nomos" was used in translating the Hebrew meaning of Torah ("law, teachings, instructions") into Greek. "Nomos" is Strong's word 3551 (see Glossary) and has the singular meaning "law" in the Greek. Thus, when the Septuagint was subsequently translated into English, "nomos" simply became the English word "law". This mistranslation of using "law" to also cover the other intended meanings (teachings, instructions) created significant problems that exist to this day. Most Christians have been taught that Yeshua replaced, or substituted, for the "law", and therefore the "law" has no relevance or application. Thus, much of the Hebrew Scriptures/Torah came to be ignored by the church for spiritual input and application, because Yahweh's teachings and instructions were effectively hidden.

Fortunately, we also have other ways for pinning down the real meaning of "law" in the New Testament. One is the Tanakh, which is a translation of the Hebrew Scriptures (Old Testament) directly from the original Hebrew text into modern English. It was produced by the Jewish Publication Society in 1985, and represents the collaboration of many academic scholars and rabbis. It therefore avoids the intermediate translation from Hebrew to Greek, and then the translation from Greek into English. It is very revealing to compare the Tanakh with the English Bible translations to see how "law" is handled.

To illustrate, the New King James Version (NKJV) of Deuteronomy 31:9-12 reads:

> [9]So Moses wrote this *LAW* and delivered it to the priests, the sons of Levi, who bore the ark of the covenant of the LORD, and to all the elders of Israel. [10]And Moses commanded them, saying: "At the end of *every* seven years, at the appointed time in the year of release, at the Feast of Tabernacles, [11]when all Israel comes to appear before the LORD your God in the place which He chooses, you shall read this *LAW* before all Israel in their hearing. [12]Gather the people together, men and women and little ones, and the stranger who *is* within your gates, that they may hear and that they may learn to fear the LORD your God and carefully observe all the words of this *LAW* (emphasis added)

Each time *LAW* is used above in the NKJV, the word *"TEACHING"* is used in the Tanakh. This further amplifies the earlier discussion that "law" as used in our English translations should also include the "teaching" (the Torah) aspect intended by the Bible. Not only is the "teaching" to be given to "all Israel" (v. 11), but it is to be given to "the stranger" (v.12). "Strangers" and "aliens" are terms used throughout the Bible to refer to gentiles. So here we see that gentiles are also to learn about and carefully observe all the words of the law (teaching or Torah).

The significance of this is further underscored in the NKJV by Deuteronomy 31:24-26:

> 24So it was, when Moses had completed writing the words of this *LAW* in a book, when they were finished, 25that Moses commanded the Levites, who bore the ark of the covenant of the LORD, saying: 26"Take this Book of the *LAW*, and put it beside the ark of the covenant of the LORD your God (emphasis added)

Again, "LAW" is used in the NKJV, but "TEACHING" is used instead of "law" in the Tanakh. Yahweh is demonstrating the importance of not bypassing the teaching aspect of His Torah.

Even the New Testament stresses this in II Timothy 3:16-17:
16All Scripture *is* given by inspiration of God, and *is* profitable for doctrine, for reproof, for correction, for instruction in righteousness, 17that the man of God may be complete, thoroughly equipped for every good work.

It is well known that "Scripture" in v. 16 refers to the Hebrew Scriptures because the New Testament was not in existence at the time Paul wrote II Timothy.

An example of where "law" means "law" is seen in Deuteronomy 4:40,44-45. The NKJV states:

> 40You shall therefore keep *His statutes and His commandments* which I command you today, that it may go well with you and with your children after you, and that you may prolong *your* days in the land which the LORD your God is giving you for all time.". . . 44Now this *is* the *law* which Moses set before the children of Israel. 45These *are* the testimonies, the statutes, and the judgments which Moses spoke to the children of Israel after they came out of Egypt, (emphasis added)

These verses in the Tanakh read:

> 40. "Observe *His laws and commandments* which I enjoin upon you this day, that it may go well with you and your children after you . . . 44. This is the *Teaching* that Moses set

before the Israelites: these are the decrees, laws, and rules that
Moses addressed to the people of Israel . . ." (emphasis added)

Thus, the Tanakh includes the concept of "law" in addition to
that of "teaching". There are numerous other passages in the
Tanakh that make distinctions between "law" and "teaching". The
point is repeated for emphasis: "law" as used in our English Bible
translations should include the "teaching and instruction" aspect,
but the church has ignored and hidden this from the very beginning.
Christians have been kept from knowing this truth ever since the
"early fathers" covered it up in their successful attempt to separate
Christianity from Judaism. The Torah *is the major building block*
that is missing in Christianity's foundation.

Another way of showing that "law" in the New Testament really
means "Torah" is through The Interlinear Bible *(5)*. In this Bible, all
words are shown in the original Hebrew and Greek along with the
English translation, and these words are numbered according to
Strong's Concordance. The translation from Hebrew to English is
based on using the Masoretic text which has preserved the original
Hebrew. It is recognized world-wide as being a "Received Text",
which means that it is highly respected among biblical scholars.

In Malachi 4:4, we see that "law" is used in the English translations (and not Torah or teaching). In the Interlinear Bible, however,
the original Hebrew uses "Torah" in place of "law". Also, we
observed above in the Tanakh that "teaching" is used instead of
"law". Therefore, when "law" is used the first time in Matthew
5:17, it is really "Torah".

We also examined Deuteronomy 31:24-26 above and saw that
each time "law" appears in the NKJV it is replaced by "teaching" in
the Tanakh. Similarly, examining these same verses in The
Interlinear Bible shows that "Torah" has replaced "law". Other
passages throughout The Interlinear show the same result: "Torah"
is used instead of "law".

It is concluded that, beyond any doubt, Yahweh's Torah is
intended for New Testament times as well as for prior times. "Law"
in the New Testament most often is referring to the "Torah". It
contains His teachings and instructions, in addition to "law".

Yeshua affirmed the Torah's fundamental importance, both in words and in modeling it for us. He obeyed it in every detail, and He asked us to obey and teach it. John 14:16 puts it rather simply: "If you love me, keep my commandments." And where were His commandments? In the Torah.

A few additional comments will complete the discussion of Matthew 5:17. Another important word to fully understand is "fulfill", which is Strong's word 4137 and has the meanings: "to complete", "to make full", "to fully preach", "to end". Clearly, in the context of Chapters 5, 6 and 7, Yeshua came to "fully preach" and interpret the Torah, not to "end" it. He loved the Torah, and He did not come to abolish it, but to fully live it out. However, many Christians have been taught the idea that Yeshua came to "fulfill" the Torah so that they do not have to. This is NOT what the Bible says.

Another important passage that connects to Yeshua's Torah theology in Matthew 5:17-20 is Matthew 28:19-20, commonly known as the Great Commission: 19 "Go therefore and make disciples of all the nations, baptizing them in the name of the Father and of the Son and of the Holy Spirit, 20 teaching them to observe all things that I have commanded you; and lo, I am with you always, even to the end of the age." Amen

Notice in v. 20 that the disciples are to "teach . . . all things that I have commanded you. . ." These "things" are none other than the commandments that Yahweh gave Yeshua in the Hebrew Scriptures/Torah. We should be taking Yeshua at His Word — studying and teaching the Torah.

A recent book by Philip Yancey, a popular Christian writer, said this about Yeshua's relationship to the Hebrew Scriptures: "When we read the Old Testament, we read the Bible Jesus read and used. These are the prayers Jesus prayed, the poems he memorized, the songs he sang, the bedtime stories he heard as a child, the prophets he pondered. He *revered every 'jot and tittle'* of the Hebrew Scriptures. The more we comprehend the Old Testament, the more we comprehend Jesus." *(6)*

If Yancey's word "revered" includes "obeyed", then his paragraph would be completely consistent with what the Bible says and what is being said here.

TORAH IN THE LIGHT
OF THE NEW COVENANT

We should also carefully review what the New Covenant says about the Torah. It was first spelled out in Jeremiah 31 and then quoted in Hebrew 8:8-12, where Yahweh says:

> 8 *"Behold, the days are coming, says the* LORD, *when I will make a new covenant with the house of Israel and with the house of Judah—9not according to the covenant that I made with their fathers in the day when I took them by the hand to lead them out of the land of Egypt; because they did not continue in My covenant, and I disregarded them, says the* LORD. *10For this is the covenant that I will make with the house of Israel after those days,* **says the** LORD: **I will put My laws (TORAH) in their mind and write them on their hearts** *(empha-sis added); and I will be their God, and they shall be My people. 11None of them shall teach his neighbor, and none his brother, saying, 'Know the* LORD,' *for all shall know Me, from the least of them to the greatest of them. 12For I will be merciful to their unrighteousness, and their sins and their lawless deeds I will remember no more."*

Let's carefully compare Hebrews 8:10 with Romans 8:1-3, which was discussed above but is repeated here for reference: *1There is* therefore now no condemnation to those who are in Christ Jesus, who do not walk according to the flesh, but according to the Spirit. **2For the law of the Spirit of life in Christ Jesus has made me free from the law of sin and death.** 3For what the law could not do in that it was weak through the flesh, God *did* by sending His own Son in the likeness of sinful flesh, on account of sin: He condemned sin in the flesh, (emphasis added)

Is "law", as used in Hebrews 8:10, the same as the "law" used in Romans 8:2? Definitely not – why would Yahweh state in Romans that Yeshua has freed us from the "law", and then turn right around and state in Hebrews that He is writing the "law" on our hearts? He would not and did not do this. There definitely has to be a difference between the "law" in Hebrews 8:10 and the "law" in Romans 8:2.

The answer is clear: the "law" of sin and death is not the "law" He writes on our hearts. The "law" in Hebrews can be none other than the "Torah", His teachings and instructions beyond the "law", which He writes on our hearts. The "law" in Romans is indeed the correct use of what law means: it is the "law of sin and death" from which Yeshua saves us.

Further, basic Christian doctrine is that the New Covenant means that "Yeshua is written on our hearts". Doing a little math gives the following equations:

> Torah is written on your heart = Hebrews 8:10 (it's Torah, not "law")
> Yeshua is written on your heart = Hebrews 8:10 (Christian doctrine)
> **Therefore Torah = Yeshua** (math axiom: things equal to the same thing are also equal)

Yes, Yeshua is the Living Torah per Hebrews 8:10, and He saved us from the "law of sin and death" per Romans 8:1-2 (and Romans 6:23: the wages of sin is death, but the gift of Yahweh is eternal life in Yeshua; and other passages). Taking one more step, Hebrews 8:13 should be reviewed:

[13]In that He says, *"A new covenant,"* He has made the first obsolete. Now what is becoming obsolete and growing old is ready to vanish away.

In the context of the above discussion, what "is becoming obsolete and . . . ready to vanish away"? ***Only the "law part" (law of sin and death) of the Torah*** in Hebrews 8:10 is becoming obsolete, because Yeshua has paid the penalty for our sin. The teaching and instruction aspect of the Torah has not become obsolete, but the church frequently uses 8:13 as a proof text to demonstrate that the "law" (Torah) is no longer relevant.

A believer and follower of Yeshua has an inner desire to please Yahweh. As the believer learns and understands more and more about the Torah, seeing what Yahweh expects, the Holy Spirit will help the believer be obedient to His teachings and instructions. The believer's goal will be to follow Yeshua's Torah lifestyle as closely as possible.

A final thought in the relationship between the Torah and the New Covenant— if we non-Jewish (gentile) believers have the Torah written in our minds and on our hearts, why are we not diligently studying the Torah right now? Why are we not preparing and rehearsing for the Millennium when we will be immersed in the Torah (Ezekiel Chapters 40-48)? Why do we offer stiff resistance when someone suggests that the Torah has spiritual input beyond just a set of "laws"?

TORAH IN THE LIGHT OF
OTHER NEW TESTAMENT PASSAGES

The foundational truth of Torah is further emphasized in James 1:22-25, which says:

> 22But be doers of the word, and not hearers only, deceiving yourselves. 23For if anyone is a hearer of the word and not a doer, he is like a man observing his natural face in a mirror; 24for he observes himself, goes away, and immediately forgets what kind of man he was. 25But he who looks into the perfect law *(TORAH)* of liberty and continues *in it,* and is not a forgetful hearer but a doer of the work, this one will be blessed in what he does. (emphasis added)

This passage is not referring to the "law of sin and death" (which Jesus saved us from), but it is pointing to the Torah, because it is the Torah that provides the *liberty* and the *blessing* in v. 25. James is emphasizing that following Yahweh's Torah gives freedom in life. The man who is obedient to the "perfect law" (Torah) will be blessed. Yahweh's blessings for Israel are enumerated in Deuteronomy 28:1-14 (and well worth reading), and many of them would also be the blessings that we can expect through Torah obedience.

Paul also emphasizes this in 1 Tim 1:8: "The 'law' (Torah) is good . . ."

Yes, the Torah is good because it is teaching and instructing in the ways of God.

Another passage that is commonly misinterpreted is Romans 10:4, which states: [4]For Christ *is* the end of the law for righteousness to everyone who believes.

Is Paul really saying that belief in Yeshua means that the "law" has ended – that it no longer applies to the Christian? "End" is the Greek word "telos", and it is Strong's word 5056. It has the primary meanings "goal", "purpose", and "end". In the *context* of what Yeshua and Paul said about the "law"(Torah) above, does "end" really fit?? Of course it doesn't. But, either "goal" or "purpose" provides excellent fits—because *YESHUA IS THE "GOAL" OF THE LAW (TORAH)*.

Yeshua made this clear in Matthew 5:17-20 as discussed above. He came to fully preach the law (Torah), to make it clear, but definitely not to end it. Yet, many Christians are taught that Romans 10:4 is a proof text showing that the "law" is finished, ended, terminated.

Many Christians also have been taught that Acts 15 relieves them from having a relationship with the Torah. The Council at Jerusalem met to discuss the important issue of what gentiles must do in order to become accepted as Christians, and after great debate, they sent a letter to the gentiles, as stated in Acts 15:28-29: [28]For it seemed good to the Holy Spirit, and to us, to lay upon you no greater burden than these necessary things: [29]that you abstain from things offered to idols, from blood, from things strangled, and from sexual immorality.

Many hold that these four requirements excluded the need for following the Torah, but this conclusion ignores the context of Acts 15 that is described in 19-21: . . . we should not trouble those from among the Gentiles who are turning to God, [20]but that we write to them to abstain from things polluted by idols, *from* sexual immorality, *from* things strangled, and *from* blood. [21]*For Moses has had throughout many generations those who preach him in every city, being read in the synagogues every Sabbath.*" (emphasis added)

The Council had concluded that they should not place additional requirements on the gentiles because they did not want to discourage them from accepting Yeshua. They knew that the Torah was ***being read in the synagogues every Sabbath***, and that the gentiles would therefore be gradually learning the Torah. Also, following these four requirements encouraged table fellowship between Jews and gentiles, which otherwise would not have been possible. The gentile was viewed as "unclean", because of eating animals sacrificed to idols and blood, and engaging in sexual promiscuity. Thus, the Torah was still in its prominent place, but the Council wisely decided not to have an immediate requirement, such as, "you must also read and obey the Torah".

Many of Paul's writings are interpreted to be anti-Torah. However, in Acts 21 he took a Nazirite vow to prove his loyalty to the Torah. This vow, as discussed in Numbers 6, was a special vow of separation made to Yahweh, and demonstrated the highest possible sincerity. He was so intent on demonstrating his love for the Torah that he also paid for four other men who were taking vows at the same time (although for different reasons).

Another example of a troublesome passage of Paul is Romans 7:4: [4]Therefore, my brethren, you also have become dead to the law through the body of Christ, that you may be married to another—to Him who was raised from the dead, that we should bear fruit to God.

This passage is troublesome to those who do not understand that "law", as used here, is only one part of the Torah. But we know that it definitely is referring to the "law of sin and death", and we are indeed *"dead to the law (of sin and death) through the body of Christ"*.

In concluding this section, it may seem that an inordinate amount of detail has been developed in showing that "law" in the New Testament must be understood as also including Yahweh's teachings and instructions, the Torah, in addition to "law". This has been intentional, because knowing the true meaning of "law" is crucial to seeing that the Hebrew Scriptures and the New Testament *really are one integrated Word from Yahweh*. We have come at the "law" versus "Torah" relationship from several different directions, and the ***evidence for each approach clearly shows that "law" in our English Bibles must include Yahweh's teachings and instructions in the Torah.***

Seeing that the Torah is the prime building block of both the Hebrew Scriptures *and the New Testament is a pivotal finding of this book.* The church's anti-Torah attitude continues to be the major divisive factor separating Christianity and Judaism, and a major cause of anti-Semitism.

CONSEQUENCES OF NOT CORRECTLY UNDERSTANDING THE TORAH

One significant consequence has been the continuing problem of not viewing the Hebrew Scriptures as an integral part of the Bible. The church accepts the historical aspects and the interesting stories in the "Old Testament", but for the most part it has discarded the aspects that affect one's lifestyle. As discussed above, the typical Christians, as taught by the church, sees the "Old Testament" as outdated "laws" that apply only to the Jewish people. For them, the Old Testament has faded away and is no longer spiritually relevant.

When all the references to the Hebrew Scriptures in the New Testament are taken into account, about 85% of the Bible *is* the Hebrew Scriptures. They are the spiritual foundation for the New Testament, yet Christianity only pays lip service to this. Many Christians know that a major theme of the Hebrew Scriptures is pointing to Yeshua, and are aware of His many citations of them during His New Testament ministry, but there is still an overriding reluctance to embrace these Scriptures spiritually. The forced separation of Christianity and Judaism, of course, prompted this situation. The impact is that, because the church has rejected the Torah, it has been robbed of the *JOY* of participating in Yahweh's feasts/appointments and His Sabbaths. It has been blinded to the benefits and blessings of a Torah-based lifestyle because it rejects the spiritual applications in the Hebrew Scriptures.

Another significant negative consequence of rejecting the Torah has been unrelenting anti-Semitism, which was addressed in the previous chapters. Or, did anti-Semitism cause the rejection of the Torah? It can be argued that, initially, anti-Semitism started with Ishmael and Esau, and that the much later rejection of the Torah then caused more anti-Semitism. Whatever the case, both have worked hand-in-hand throughout history to create problems.

Other countries have historically tried to blame all problems on the Jews, which ultimately gives rise to trying to destroy them. Even today, most of the world through the United Nations blames Israel for the Middle East problems. Other nations turn Israel's self-defense against terrorism around, and it becomes an invasion of the "poor Palestinians". The Bible says that in the end times "evil will be called good and good will be called evil" (Isaiah 5:20). World attitudes toward Israel confirm this.

Rejecting the Torah is also causing problems for the church. Slowly but surely, it seems that the church is having a continually decreasing impact in bringing about a visible improvement in righteous living. The world is becoming worse – not better. Extreme dishonesty and fraud in corporate executive ranks, the travesty of molestation in the Catholic Church, lust of money among professional athletes, abortion, homosexuality, and deception by politicians are just a few examples of a society starting to spin out of control. Why isn't the church having some kind of positive effect? Has it been stunted because it rejected Yahweh's Torah?

Luke 6:46: "But why do you call me 'Lord, Lord,' and not do the things which I say?"

(Lord . . . do You mean obey the Torah?)

Matthew 15:9 But in vain do they worship me, Teaching as their doctrines the precepts of men

How odd of God to choose the Jew,
But not so odd as those who choose
The Jewish God and hate the Jew. (Author unknown) (. . . and therefore hate the Torah??)

Jeremiah 16:11 what *is* our sin that we have committed against the LORD our God? [11]Then shalt thou say unto them, Because your fathers have forsaken me, saith the LORD, and have walked after other gods, and have served them, and have worshipped them, and have forsaken me, and have not kept my law *(TORAH)*

I love to tell the story of unseen things above;
Of Jesus and His glory, of Jesus and His love.
I love to tell the story, twill be my theme in glory;
To tell the old, old story, of Jesus and His love.

5. THE TRUTH ABOUT THE SABBATH and INTRODUCTION TO YAHWEH'S APPOINTMENTS

━━━━►∘◄━━━━

Leviticus 26:30 — And I will destroy your high places, *and cut down your sun-images* (emphasis added), and cast your dead bodies upon the bodies of your idols; and my soul shall abhor you.

Ezekiel 8:16-17 — [16]So He brought me into the inner court of the LORD'S house; and there . . . were about twenty-five men with their backs toward the temple of the LORD and their faces toward the east, and *they were worshiping the sun toward the east.* (emphasis added) [17]And He said to me, "Have you seen this, O son of man . . . the abominations which they commit here?

Mark 7:8 — For laying aside the commandment of God, you hold the tradition of men.

The Torah is fundamental to biblical Christianity for reasons discussed in Chapter 4, and it also provides the means for correctly understanding and interpreting Yahweh's important appointments in Leviticus 23. For those who come to see that Yahweh wants all believers to find spiritual value in the Hebrew Scriptures/Torah, there then follows close behind a *desire* to observe His appointments.

Leviticus 23:1-2 states: [1]And the LORD spoke to Moses, saying, [2]"Speak to the children of Israel, and say to them: 'The feasts of the LORD, which you shall proclaim *to be* holy convocations, these *are* My feasts.

These first two verses are the introduction to the rest of the chapter, and they are packed with important information. Some other versions of the Bible include the word "appointed" just before "feasts", so we are dealing here with Yahweh's appointed feasts – these are *His appointments* – they are not "Jewish things".

In verse 2, "children of Israel" was initially intended for the physical Israelites who had come out of Egypt in the Exodus, but it is also appropriate for "children of Israel", or "Israelites", to be applied in the spiritual sense. After all, Galatians 3:29 states that we are Abraham's seed: [29]And if you *are* Christ's, then you are Abraham's seed, and heirs according to the promise.

Also, the entire Chapter 1 of Matthew lays out the genealogy from Abraham through Yeshua. If we are *spiritual* heirs of Yeshua, we are also *spiritual* heirs of Abraham. Therefore, it seems logical to conclude that, in a *spiritual* sense, all believers are being addressed in v. 2, as well as the physical "children of Israel". Some will vehemently declare that Christians are not included as part of the "children of Israel", and they will bend over backwards trying to prove this. Is it possible that ant-Semitism, nurtured by the church for centuries, is the root cause as to why many Christians do not want to have association with the Jews – or have anything to do with the Torah?

"Proclaim" in Leviticus 23:2 is Strong's word 7122 and has the meanings "invite" and "preach". The children of Israel are being asked by Yahweh to invite others, including gentiles, to join His "holy convocations". "Convocation" is the Hebrew word *miqra*, which means "rehearsal" or "assembly". Yahweh wants it to be proclaimed to everyone that His holy feasts are "rehearsals". Rehearsals for what? In a following chapter we will see that not only do His appointments rehearse and proclaim what Yeshua has already done for us, and what He will do for us when He returns, but they also are rehearsals for what we will be doing in the Millennium.

Further, it is re-emphasized that these are *HIS* appointments. These are "Yahweh-things", not "Jewish things", as the church believes. Leviticus (written around 1400 BC) is addressing Hebrews and the "mixed multitude" (Exodus 12:38) who had fled Egypt. The "mixed multitude" would have consisted of many gentile Egyptians who had come to faith in Yahweh, and probably gentiles from other countries, as a result of seeing Yahweh make a mockery of Egypt's gods. It is emphasized repeatedly herein that the designation "Jews" did not come into existence for another five or so centuries. II Kings 16:5-6 states:

> ⁵Then Rezin king of Syria and Pekah the son of Remaliah,
> king of Israel, came up to Jerusalem to make war; and they
> besieged Ahaz but could not overcome him. ⁶At that time
> Rezin king of Syria captured Elath for Syria, and drove the
> *MEN OF JUDAH* (emphasis added) from Elath.

The context here is the period after Israel split around 970 BC into the Northern Kingdom of Israel/Ephraim and the Southern Kingdom of Judah. It was only then that people in the Southern Kingdom came to be known as "men of Judah", or as "Jews" (in the King James Version). In the Tanakh, they were known as "Judites". So Yahweh is not inviting only Jews – He is inviting everyone to join in HIS appointments.

WHAT OTHERS HAVE SAID ABOUT THE SABBATH

It is important to see the spiritual significance that Yeshua attached to the Sabbath and the annual appointments. Dr. John Garr expresses it very well: "The Sabbath and the agricultural festivals took on spiritual significance. First of all, Jesus became the Sabbath for all believers (Hebrews 4:1-11). He also became the Passover to those who received Him (1 Corinthians 5:7). Pentecost became a time for celebrating the giving of the Holy Spirit as well as the giving of the Torah. . . the system of Judaism was not destroyed: it was merely reformed. Celebration of the Sabbath and of the festivals continued in remembrance of the Lord of the Sabbath and of

His works of redemption (Passover) and empowerment (Pentecost). Without exception, the work of Jesus was one of reformation of the existing system of Judaism, not of its abrogation and replacement with a completely new system called Christianity." *(1)*

The Sabbath is the first appointment listed in Leviticus 23, and verse 3 states: [3]'Six days shall work be done, but the seventh day *is* a Sabbath of solemn rest, a holy convocation. You shall do no work *on it;* it *is* the Sabbath of the LORD in all your dwellings.

Many Christians believe that the holy Sabbath ordained by Yahweh no longer applies, and that Sunday is now the "Christian Sabbath". This is not what the Bible says. Changing the day of worship from the Sabbath to Sunday came very early in the process of the church separating from its Hebraic roots. Philip Schaff's church history states the following:

"The fathers did not regard the Christian Sunday as continuation of, but as a substitute for, the Jewish Sabbath. . . There was a disposition to disparage the Jewish law in the zeal to prove the independent originality of Christian institutions. The same polemic interest against Judaism ruled in the paschal controversies, and made Christian Easter a movable feast. . . Ignatius was the first who contrasted Sunday with the Jewish Sabbath as something done away with. . . Tertullian, at the close of the second and beginning of the third century, views the Lord's Day as figurative of rest from sin and typical of man's final rest, and says: 'We have nothing to do with Sabbaths, new moons or the Jewish festivals . . .'"*(2)*

Emperor Constantine made "official" the substitution of Sunday for the Sabbath in 321: "The emperor Constantine, a convert to Christianity, introduced the first civil legislation concerning Sunday in 321, when he decreed that all work should cease on Sunday, except that farmers could work if necessary. This law, aimed at providing time for worship, was followed later in the same century and in subsequent centuries by further restrictions on Sunday activities." (*Encyclopedia Britannica*, 15th Edition, p. 672)

And Jesse Hurlbut in his history of Christianity said: "As long as the church was mainly Jewish, the Hebrew Sabbath was kept; but as soon as it became increasingly gentile the first day (Sunday) gradually took the place of the seventh day (Saturday)." *(3)*

Cristopher O'Quin in a First Fruits of Zion publication also points out: "The writings of Ignatius around 107 stated that Sabbath services were considered part of "obsolete practices" and believers were coerced to change their calendars in accordance with "the Lord's Day". In the Epistle of Mathetes, written around 130, Jewish practices in accordance with the Torah are condemned in no uncertain terms: 'But again their scruples concerning meats, and their superstition relating to the Sabbath and the vanity of their circumcision . . . I suppose you do not need to learn from me, are ridiculous and unworthy of any consideration.' " *(4)*

We should worship Yahweh on every day of the week, but the Bible makes it clear that the Sabbath (Saturday) is the 7th day, and that it alone is His appointed holy day of rest which is to be observed forever. The passages discussed in the next section show why the Sabbath is to be observed today and in the future. Removal of the Sabbath from the Christian worship was entirely a man-ordained political decision, and it is completely contrary to Yahweh's Bible.

YAHWEH CLEARLY COMMANDED
SABBATH OBSERVANCE

Yahweh said right after everything was created that the seventh day was holy and was to be the day of rest for all mankind. Genesis 2:1-3 states:

> [1]Thus the heavens and the earth, and all the host of them, were finished. [2]And on the seventh day God ended His work which He had done, and He rested on the seventh day from all His work which He had done. [3]Then God blessed the seventh day and sanctified it, because in it He rested from all His work which God had created and made.

It is clear from several passages that the 7th day of the week is the Sabbath and that Sunday is the first day of the week (Matthew 28:1, Luke 23:54-24:1, John 20:1). The Bible does not support the idea that Sunday is the "Christian Sabbath". For example, Matthew

28:1 states: [1]Now after the Sabbath, as the first *day* of the week began to dawn, Mary Magdalene and the other Mary came to see the tomb.

Yahweh also states in the 4th Commandment to remember the Sabbath and keep it holy. Exodus 20:8-11 states:

> "Remember the Sabbath day, to keep it holy. [9]Six days you shall labor and do all your work, [10]but the seventh day *is* the Sabbath of the LORD your God. *In it* you shall do no work: you, nor your son, nor your daughter, nor your male servant, nor your female servant, nor your cattle, nor your stranger who *is* within your gates. [11]For *in* six days the LORD made the heavens and the earth, the sea, and all that *is* in them, and rested the seventh day. Therefore the LORD blessed the Sabbath day and hallowed it.

He also made it clear that the Sabbath will exist even at the future time of His creating the new heavens and earth. Isaiah 66:22-23 states:

> [22]"For as the new heavens and the new earth Which I will make shall remain before Me," says the LORD,
> "So shall your descendants and your name remain. [23]And it shall come to pass
> *That* from one New Moon to another, And from one Sabbath to another,
> All flesh shall come to worship before Me," says the LORD.

Yeshua confirmed that the Sabbath will exist in the future; the cross did not cancel it as many believe. Matthew 24:19-21 states:

> 19 But woe to those who are pregnant and to those who are nursing babies in those days! 20 And pray that your flight may not be in winter or on the Sabbath. 21 For then there will be great tribulation, such as has not been since the beginning of the world until this time, no, nor ever shall be.

A Sabbath rest for the "people of God" is clearly described in

Hebrews Chapter 4, showing beyond any doubt that the Sabbath is intended for both Jewish and non-Jewish believers. Hebrews 4:9-12 states:

> [9]There remains therefore a rest for the people of God. [10]For he who has entered His rest has himself also ceased from his works as God *did* from His. [11]Let us therefore be diligent to enter that rest, lest anyone fall according to the same example of disobedience. [12]For the word of God *is* living and powerful, and sharper than any two-edged sword, piercing even to the division of soul and spirit, and of joints and marrow, and is a discerner of the thoughts and intents of the heart.

And Yeshua said in Mark2:27: [27]And He said to them, "The Sabbath was made for man, and not man for the Sabbath. 28 Therefore the Son of Man is also Lord of the Sabbath."

Yahweh said that all believers will find *joy* in Him if we will honor the Sabbath.

Isaiah 58:13-14 states:

> [13]If you turn away your foot from the Sabbath, F*rom* doing
>   your pleasure on My holy day,
> And call the Sabbath a delight, The holy *day* of the LORD
>   honorable,
> And shall honor Him, not doing your own ways, Nor finding
>   your own pleasure,
> Nor speaking *your own* words, [14]Then you shall delight your-
>   self in the LORD;
> And I will cause you to ride on the high hills of the earth, And
>   feed you with the heritage of Jacob your father.
> The mouth of the LORD has spoken."

He also emphasized that gentiles will find special *joy* in keeping the Sabbath.

Isaiah 56:6-7 states:

> [6]Also the sons of the foreigner, Who join themselves to the

LORD, to serve Him,
And to love the name of the LORD, to be His servants—
Everyone who keeps from defiling the Sabbath,
And holds fast My covenant— [7]Even them I will bring to My
holy mountain,

And make them joyful in My house of prayer. Their burnt
offerings and their sacrifices
Will be accepted on My altar; For My house shall be called a
house of prayer for all nations."(emphasis added)

Ezekiel Chapters 40-48 are perhaps the most detailed passages in the Bible describing the Millennium. Following are several verses among many showing that the Sabbath will be observed at this time. Ezekiel 46 states:

[1]'Thus says the Lord GOD: "The gateway of the inner court that faces toward the east shall be shut the six working days; but on the Sabbath it shall be opened, and on the day of the New Moon it shall be opened. . .
[3]Likewise the people of the land shall worship at the entrance to this gateway before the LORD on the Sabbaths and the New Moons. . .

The "new moon" is the beginning of a new month in the biblical calendar.

YESHUA AND HIS APOSTLES
FAITHFULLY OBSERVED THE SABBATH

In addition to the above passages, there are numerous instances in the New Testament showing that Yeshua and the disciples honored the Sabbath, as well as the other appointments of God in Leviticus 23. Luke 4:14-16 states:

[14]Then Jesus returned in the power of the Spirit to Galilee, and news of Him went out through all the surrounding region.

15And He taught in their synagogues, being glorified by all. 16So He came to Nazareth, where He had been brought up. And *as His custom was*, He went into the synagogue on the Sabbath day, and stood up to read. (emphasis added)

In the context of Acts 15, James and other leaders knew well that gentiles would be keeping the Sabbath in the synagogues to learn more about God's Torah:

Acts 15: 19"It is my judgment, therefore, that we should not make it difficult for the Gentiles who are turning to God. 20Instead we should write to them, telling them to abstain from food polluted by idols, from sexual immorality, from the meat of strangled animals and from blood. 21For Moses has been preached in every city from the earliest times and is read in the synagogues on every Sabbath."

We see that Paul went to Sabbath services where there were both Jews and gentiles. This was *his custom, as it was Yeshua's:*

Acts 17: 1When they had passed through Amphipolis and Apollonia, they came to Thessalonica, where there was a Jewish synagogue. 2*As his custom* was, Paul went into the synagogue, and *on three Sabbath* days he reasoned with them from the Scriptures, 3explaining and proving that the Christ had to suffer and rise from the dead. "This Jesus I am proclaiming to you is the Christ" he said. 4Some of the Jews were persuaded and joined Paul and Silas, as did a large number of *God-fearing Greeks (gentiles)* and not a few prominent women. (emphasis added)

The Book of Acts cites some 80 times that the disciples observed the Sabbath and attended Sabbath services. For example, Acts 13:13-15 states:

13From Paphos, Paul and his companions sailed to Perga in Pamphylia, where John left them to return to Jerusalem.

14From Perga they went on to Pisidian Antioch. *On the Sabbath* they entered the synagogue and sat down. 15After the reading from the Law and the Prophets, the synagogue rulers sent word to them, saying, "Brothers, if you have a message of encouragement for the people, please speak."

God simply did not have different rules or standards for the Jews and gentiles. The Sabbath was intended for both. Galatians 3:28-29 affirms this:

28**There is neither Jew nor Greek, slave nor free, male nor female, for you are all one in Christ Jesus.** 29**If you belong to Christ, then you are Abraham's seed, and heirs according to the promise.**

Therefore, in light of the above passages, how can the church honestly conclude that the Sabbath is no longer in effect and that Sunday has replaced it? Or, conclude that the Leviticus 23 appointments were cancelled? Nothing in the Bible supports these conclusions. On the contrary, Yahweh created the Sabbath as His holy day of rest, Yeshua reconfirmed this, and both of them stated clearly that the Sabbath would exist in the future. Clearly, the church has hidden the truth of the Sabbath for 1900 years, and Christians have been led astray.

Perhaps the most revealing question of all is this: Why is it that the Sabbath was observed in ancient Israel, and continued being observed through Yeshua's and the apostles' ministries; *but then is NOT being observed in the so-called present "church age";* only to once again be observed in the Millennium?? Who decided that there should be a church age gap of over 1900 years during which time the Sabbath does not apply to gentile believers? Neither Yahweh nor Yeshua ever said that Sunday would be observed instead of the Sabbath during the church age. The answer is that the early "church fathers" decided that replacing the Sabbath with Sunday was another good way to separate Christianity from Judaism.

COMMONLY MISINTERPRETED PASSAGES

The church, starting in earlier centuries, has also misinterpreted passages of Paul to rationalize substituting Sunday for the Sabbath. Following is a discussion of some of the major passages used to "justify" (rationalize) the substitution:

Romans 14:5-6:

> [5]One person esteems *one* day above another; another esteems every day *alike*. Let each be fully convinced in his own mind. [6]He who observes the day, observes *it* to the Lord; and he who does not observe the day, to the Lord he does not observe *it*. He who eats, eats to the Lord, for he gives God thanks; and he who does not eat, to the Lord he does not eat, and gives God thanks.

Many Christians have been taught that these verses refer to the Sabbath, with the implication that it is acceptable to substitute Sunday for it. However, the Sabbath is not mentioned even one time in all of Chapter 14. The context of the chapter is all about eating – not the Sabbath. Numerous times throughout the chapter "eating" is the topic of the passages.

The real context is about food sacrificed to idols, and 1 Corinthians 8 is applicable. Verses 7-13 state:

> [7]However, there is not in everyone that knowledge; for some, with consciousness of the idol, until now eat *it* as a thing offered to an idol; and their conscience, being weak, is defiled. [8]But food does not commend us to God; for neither if we eat are we the better, nor if we do not eat are we the worse. [9]But beware lest somehow this liberty of yours become a *stumbling block* to those who are weak. [10]For if anyone sees you who have knowledge eating in an idol's temple, will not the conscience of him who is weak be emboldened to eat those things offered to idols? [11]And because of your knowledge shall the weak brother perish, for whom Christ died? [12]But when you thus sin against the brethren, and wound their weak

conscience, you sin against Christ. [13]Therefore, if *food makes my brother stumble*, I will never again eat meat, *lest I make my brother stumble*. (emphasis added)

The above verses are focusing on causing a brother to stumble, and are very similar to Romans 14:13-15:

[13]Therefore let us not judge one another anymore, but rather resolve this, not to put a *stumbling block* (emphasis added) or a cause to fall in our brother's way. [14]I know and am convinced by the Lord Jesus that *there is* nothing unclean of itself; but to him who considers anything to be unclean, to him *it is* unclean. [15]Yet if your brother is grieved because of *your* food, you are no longer walking in love. Do not destroy with your food the one for whom Christ died.

The "therefore" in v.13 refers to what has taken place in earlier verses, and those earlier verses are talking about eating food so as not to make a brother stumble, just as 1 Corinthians 8 is concerned about a "stumbling block". These verses are not in any way referring to the Sabbath.

Even if the reader does not understand or agree with the above, the overriding reason why Romans 14:5 does not refer to the Sabbath is because, if it did, Paul would be in total opposition to Yeshua's teachings and actions. This cannot be. Paul was known for being a faithful apostle of Yeshua, who honored the Sabbath as "a matter of custom". Paul would not have contradicted Yeshua on the matter of the Sabbath, or any other issue.

Acts 20:7:

[7]Now on the first *day* of the week, when the disciples came together to break bread, Paul, ready to depart the next day, spoke to them and continued his message until midnight. [8]There were many lamps in the upper room where they were gathered together.

Many hold that this verse shows worship on Sunday. However, if we remember that the first day of the week, Sunday, is from sundown Saturday evening to sundown on Sunday, we see that Paul was meeting with them Saturday and not conducting a church service on Sunday. This gathering was really a going away party for Paul. "The many lamps" in v. 8 further confirms that their meeting continued into Saturday night. Later, in v. 11, it is stated that Paul talked until daylight (early Sunday morning) and then departed. Acts 20:7 does not in any way imply that this was a church service on Sunday morning.

1 Cor 16:2:

> Now concerning the collection for the saints, as I have given
> orders to the churches of Galatia, so you must do also: ²On
> the first *day* of the week let each one of you lay something
> aside, storing up as he may prosper, that there be no collec-
> tions when I come.

Many hold that this was a Sunday collection during church services. However, the context is that these collections were to help those who had suffered famine (See Acts 11:27-30, Romans 15:26, and 2 Corinthians 8:1-5), and Paul was asking them to set aside a portion of the money made during the preceding week. Money would not have been collected on the Sabbath in any case. The Sabbath had ended at sundown, and that evening would be a logical time to figure their earnings during the week. This was not a Sunday church collection, but rather a collection to help others. In Nehemiah 10:31, Israelites were commanded not to buy or sell on the Sabbath. The rabbis later extended this to mean not to handle money at all on the Sabbath.

Colossians 2:16 :

> ¹⁶So let no one judge you in food or in drink, or regarding a
> festival or a new moon or sabbaths, ¹⁷which are a shadow of
> things to come, but the substance is of Christ.

Most Christians have been taught that Colossians Chapter 2, and particularly 2:16, is a proof-text for showing that Christians do not need to observe the Sabbath or the festivals in Leviticus Chapter 23. Once again the problem of CONTEXT arises in understanding some of the difficult statements of Paul. In Colossians 2, Paul is encouraging new believers not to let heathens (outsiders) dissuade them from following Yeshua, and not to let heathens judge them for keeping the Sabbath and feasts. The "you" in the preceding verses leading up to v. 16 is referring to NEW believers, so *v.16 is not referring to believers judging one another.* The "one" in this verse is referring to an unbeliever. Substituting "unbeliever" for "one" and "new believer" for "you" gives the intended meaning of v.16: "So let no *unbeliever* judge you, *new believer*, in food or in drink . . ."

Paul is encouraging new believers to participate in the festivals (Yahweh's appointments) and the Sabbath because they are "a shadow" of Yeshua. They are rehearsals for the infinite number of times we will be celebrating the Sabbath and the festivals with Yeshua after He returns. Ezekiel Chapters 40-48 clearly describe that we will be celebrating them in the Millennium.

The fact is that the Bible mentions "Sabbath" over 160 times and Sunday not once. This alone should create suspicion that something is wrong. Yeshua never changed the Sabbath to Sunday—early church "fathers" did. On the contrary, He and His followers honored it throughout the New Testament as the 7th day of the week, and Sunday is clearly the 1st day of the week.

If you, the reader, do not accept the explanations given for the above passages, answer these questions for yourself: Why would Paul — who acknowledged the goodness and holiness of the Torah (Romans 7:12) and who faithfully kept the Sabbath and the festivals – be telling believers that it was not important for them to do so? Why would he be telling them that Sunday was substituted for the 7th day Sabbath and then turn right around and as a matter of custom honor the Sabbath himself? *It would have made no sense whatsoever for him to do the opposite of what he preached.*

In this chapter we have seen that Yahweh shows in passage after passage how important the Sabbath is to Him. Yeshua and the apostles observed the Sabbath as "was their custom" throughout early

New Testament times. If we are really trying to conform to Yeshua's Torah-based lifestyle, then following His example of observing the Sabbath seems to be something that we can do. The early "church fathers", however, in their continuing efforts to separate Christianity from its Hebrew roots, arbitrarily decided that they wanted Sun-day instead of Yahweh's Sabbath, and led the church away from observing it.

The church itself has admitted that there has been no scriptural authority for substituting Sunday for the Sabbath. Here are three examples: the Catholic Press, August 25, 1900 stated: "Sunday is a Catholic institution, and . . . can be defended only on Catholic principles . . . From beginning to end of Scripture there is not a single passage that warrants the transfer of weekly public worship from the last day of the week to the first." The Methodist Church *(5)* has stated: "Sabbath in the Hebrew language signifies rest, and is the seventh day of the week . . . and it must be confessed that there is no law in the New Testament concerning the first day." The Baptist Church *(6)* said — "There is nothing in Scripture that requires us to keep Sunday rather than Saturday as a holy day."

Summarizing, no interpretation of nebulous Bible passages is needed in order to conclude that the substitution of Sunday for Yahweh's Sabbath was blatantly wrong – the Bible spells it out clearly that His holy day of rest and worship is the Sabbath, the 7th day. This should be the most easily understood topic in the Bible, but it has been made difficult and complex by the church.

We of finite minds will have to await being with Him in heaven before having a full understanding of all that His Sabbath encompasses. But for now, when we have His written Word that commands observance of the Sabbath, what will be the response when He asks: "Why did you not obey me?" An answer like, "the church told me it was Sunday", is not going to work. We need to read and obey the Bible for ourselves – not depend on a church corrupted by paganism to interpret it for us.

6. THE APPOINTMENTS (FEASTS) OF YAHWEH

———⇒>⋅⊙⋅<⇐———

Jeremiah 7: [16]"Therefore do not pray for this people, nor lift up a cry or prayer for them, nor make intercession to Me; for I will not hear you. [17]Do you not see what they do in the cities of Judah and in the streets of Jerusalem? [18]The children gather wood, the fathers kindle the fire, and the women knead dough, to make cakes *for the queen of heaven*; and *they* pour out drink offerings to other gods, *that they may provoke Me to anger*. (emphasis added)
(honoring the goddess Easter)

As mentioned in the previous chapters, the Torah is fundamental to biblical Christianity, and it provides the way for correctly interpreting Yahweh's important appointments in Leviticus 23. These are *His* appointed feasts, and He ordained them not to be burdensome, but to be times of joy with His people. He intends these appointments to be rehearsals for the times we celebrate them with Him in the Millennium (Ezekiel Chapters 40-48). But, even more importantly in the present day, they also commemorate what Yeshua has already done for us through His first coming, and what He will do for us when He returns.

The discussion in this chapter is limited to show specifically how each of the Leviticus 23 feasts points to Yeshua; it does not cover the many other interesting facets of them. Yahweh wants to meet with us at *His* holy assemblies, which are to be "proclaimed" to everyone. It is indeed ironic that the church, which rightly **wants** to celebrate Yeshua, has rejected the very section of the Bible that is all about honoring Him: Yahweh's Leviticus 23 appointments. Here again the church is guilty of leading Christians away from the truth of the Torah.

Christians who have come to observe *His* appointments are experiencing the joy which Yahweh describes in Isaiah 56:6-7:

> [6]"Also the **sons of the foreigner** Who join themselves to the
>   LORD, to serve Him,
> And to love the name of the LORD, to be His servants—
> Everyone who keeps from defiling the Sabbath, **And holds
>   fast My covenant**—
> [7]Even them I will bring to My holy mountain, And **make them
>   joyful** in My house of prayer.
> Their burnt offerings and their sacrifices *Will be* accepted on
>   My altar;
> For My house shall be called a house of prayer for all nations."
>   (emphasis added)

Gentiles (*"sons of foreigners"*, v.6) who follow His Torah (*"holds fast My covenant"*, v.6) will find joy in His house (*"make them joyful in my house"*, v.7). This is just one more example showing the fundamental importance of seeing the spiritual applications for Christians in the Torah. *His* Leviticus 23 appointments are a centerpiece of *His* Torah, and yet the church has missed the joy of seeing Yeshua in them.

THE PASSOVER WEEK

Passover week consists of the day of Passover (Nisan 14), the week of unleavened bread which starts the day after Passover (Nisan 15-22), and First Fruits which is the day when the barley crop in Israel becomes *abib* (ready for harvest). Nisan, the first month of the year on the biblical calendar, corresponds to the March-April period on the Gregorian calendar. The biblical calendar is based on the lunar cycle, while the Gregorian calendar is based on the solar cycle. Passover week is described in Leviticus 23:4-10:

> [4]'These *are* the feasts of the LORD, holy convocations which you shall proclaim at their appointed times. [5]On the fourteenth *day* of the first month at twilight *is* the LORD'S Passover. [6]And on the fifteenth day of the same month *is* the Feast of Unleavened Bread to the LORD; seven days you must eat unleavened bread. [7]On the first day you shall have a holy convocation; you shall do no customary work on it. [8]But you shall offer an offering made by fire to the LORD for seven days. The seventh day *shall be* a holy convocation; you shall do no customary work *on it.*'"
>
> [9]And the LORD spoke to Moses, saying, [10]"Speak to the children of Israel, and say to them: 'When you come into the land which I give to you, and reap its harvest, then you shall bring a sheaf of the firstfruits of your harvest to the priest.

On Passover night, Yahweh had them put blood from their sacrificed lambs on their doorposts so that their firstborn would not die when His angel of death "passed over" Egypt.

Exodus 12:12-15 states:

> [12]'For I will pass through the land of Egypt on that night, and will strike all the firstborn in the land of Egypt, both man and beast; and against all the gods of Egypt I will execute judgment: I *am* the LORD. [13]Now the blood shall be a sign for you on the houses where you *are.* And when I see the blood, I will pass over you; and the plague shall not be on you to destroy *you* when I strike the land of Egypt. [14]'So this day shall be to you a memorial; and you shall keep it as a feast to the LORD throughout your generations. You shall keep it as a feast by an everlasting ordinance. [15]Seven days you shall eat unleavened bread.

The blood of their sacrificed lambs saved their firstborn as they hurriedly departed Egypt. For Christians, it is the lamb of Yahweh,

Yeshua, whose blood was applied to the doorposts of our hearts in order to save us from our sin. Israel was delivered from slavery in Egypt, and Christians were delivered from their slavery to sin. 1 Corinthians 5:7 states: [7]Therefore purge out the old leaven, that you may be a new lump, since you truly are unleavened. For indeed Christ, our Passover, was sacrificed for us.

YESHUA WAS SACRIFICED
AT SAME TIME OF DAY AS PASSOVER LAMBS

Yeshua, our Passover Lamb, was sacrificed for us at the same time, twilight, on the same day, Nisan 14, as the Israelites' lambs were sacrificed.

Yeshua was on the cross from 12 noon (the 6th hour) until 3 pm (the 9th hour), when He died (Matthew 27:45). This took place on the Day of Preparation (Nisan 13) which was just before the Passover was celebrated on Nisan 14 (Leviticus 23:5; John 19:31). **Remember, Nisan 14 started at sundown on the DAY of Preparation.** He was buried by Joseph of Arimathea and Nicodemus late in the Day of Preparation because the Jewish people did not want His body on the cross during Passover (John 19:31-42).

The Passover lambs were sacrificed at twilight on Nisan 14 (Exodus12:6). Twilight is generally understood to be the few hours just before sundown. So Yeshua was crucified at the same time the lambs were sacrificed for the first Passover after leaving Egypt.

YESHUA WAS RESURRECTED ON THE SABBATH

It is important to determine when He was resurrected. Mary found the tomb empty when she went there early in the morning, *when it was still dark*, on Sunday the 1st day of the week (John 20:1). Yeshua had said that He would be in the grave three days and three nights (Matthew12:40). Nisan 14 was the 1st night and 1st day; Nisan 15 was the 2d night and day; and Nisan 16 was the 3rd night and day. Therefore, He was resurrected sometime during the daylight hours of Nisan 16, which preceded the time Mary found the tomb empty early Sunday morning when it was still dark. So, *He was resurrected on the Sabbath, the 7th day.* He could not have been resurrected on Sunday because then He would have been in the grave 4 nights, violating Matthew 12:40.

It is also worth noting that Yeshua's triumphal entry into Jerusalem was on or about Nisan 10 (John 12; Matthew 21). He was, in effect, on display before the people of Israel, when He spoke in the temple and was questioned by the priests. Similarly, the Passover lambs were selected by the priests on Nisan 10 after being checked for defects (Exodus12:3-5). Thus, both Yeshua and the lambs were on display for four days before they were crucified and sacrificed, respectively.

WHERE DOES EASTER FIT IN?

The Council of Nicea, convened by Constantine, was discussed in Chapter 2. The Council ruled that Easter would replace Passover and be celebrated on the first Sunday occurring after the first full moon and the first day of spring. Easter is the name of an ancient fertility goddess of both springtime and offspring (hence, bunnies and eggs). The Canaanites, the pagan people who occupied the Holy Land prior to the Israelites, worshiped her as the Queen of Heaven, Astarte, although other cultures had different names for her; for example, she was "Ishtar" in Assyria. Note what Jeremiah 7:17-18 says:

> [7]Do you not see what they do in the cities of Judah and in the streets of Jerusalem? [18]The children gather wood, the fathers kindle the fire, and the women knead dough, to make cakes for the *queen of heaven* (emphasis added)

The pagan rite of Easter became a part of 2nd century Christianity as a compromise with the Christian celebration of Yeshua's resurrection at First Fruits during Passover week. That is, worship of Easter and His resurrection were blended together in order to placate pagans entering Christianity.

The historical literature is abundant in showing the pagan

origins of Easter. Even the encyclopedias plainly show the pagan connection:

- "As at Christmas, so also at Easter, popular customs reflect many ancient pagan survivals. In this instance, connected with spring fertility rites, are such symbols as the Easter egg and the Easter rabbit." (Easter: Britannica Online 1996)
- ". . . the name Easter is derived from the pagan spring festival of the goddess Eostre, and many folk customs (Easter eggs, for ex.) are of pagan origin."
  (Easter: The 1995 Grolier Multimedia Enc.)

Today when we look back on the fact that Easter, a pagan rite through and through, was substituted for the events of Passover week, commemorating Yeshua's sacrifice and resurrection, it seems incredulous that Easter remains the church's choice for remembering the most significant events in biblical Christianity. We observed in Chapter 2 the charged political and anti-Semitic atmosphere at the Council of Nicea in 325 when the substitution of Easter for Passover was made "official". How could the so-called Protestant Reformation in the 1500s fail to extinguish this grossest of errors? One reason, of course, is that the leader of the reformation, Martin Luther, became a vicious anti-Semitist on a par with the "church fathers".

UNLEAVENED BREAD AND FIRST FRUITS

To complete the picture of Passover week, during the seven days of Unleavened Bread Yahweh commanded that only bread without yeast be eaten. Yeast in the Bible represents sin, so eating bread without yeast symbolized that Yeshua was sinless and was our bread of life. Note
I Corinthians 5:6-7:

> [6]Your glorying *is* not good. Do you not know that a little leaven leavens the whole lump? [7]Therefore purge out the old leaven, that you may be a new lump, since you truly are

unleavened. For indeed Christ, our Passover, was sacrificed
for us.

Dr. John Garr provides an interesting comment on what removing the leaven from our lives means: "The fact that the removal of leaven is both an event of one day and of seven additional days helps us to understand that believers in Christ initially have sin removed from their lives by the shed blood of the Passover Lamb and that the purification process is one which extends through time in a sanctification process which is manifest in obedience to the Word of God (John 17:17; Ephesians 5:26)." *(1)*

First Fruits reminds us that we will be raised in newness of life with Him. Romans 6:4 states:

> Therefore we were buried with Him through baptism into
> death, that just as Christ was raised from the dead by the glory
> of the Father, even so we also should walk in newness of life.

Yahweh's third appointment during Passover week, the festival of First Fruits, celebrated the fertility of the land by bringing the first fruits of the barley harvest and presenting them to Him. Yeshua was resurrected on the day of First Fruits, as stated in 1 Corinthians 15:20: But now Christ is risen from the dead, and has become the firstfruits of those who have fallen asleep.

Summarizing Passover week, we see that it commemorates Yeshua's death, burial, and resurrection. The believer who observes the Passover appointments is remembering what He did for us during His first ministry.

FEAST OF WEEKS (Pentecost)

The Feast of Weeks (Pentecost) occurs 50 days after First Fruits and celebrates the first fruits of the wheat harvest. For Israel, this feast remembers that 50 days after the Exodus the Israelites reached Mt. Sinai where Yahweh gave them the Torah. It was also being given to the many gentiles who had attached themselves to Israel because they wanted to follow Yahweh.

Leviticus 23:15-16 states: And you shall count for yourselves from the day after the Sabbath, from the day that you brought the sheaf of the wave offering: seven Sabbaths shall be completed. 16. Count fifty days to the day after the seventh Sabbath; then you shall offer a new grain offering to the LORD.

For believers in Yeshua, 50 days after the resurrection of Yeshua they were given the Holy Spirit, as Acts 2:1-4 describes:

> [1]When the Day of Pentecost had fully come, they were all with one accord in one place. [2]And suddenly there came a sound from heaven, as of a rushing mighty wind, and it filled the whole house where they were sitting. [3]Then there appeared to them divided tongues, as of fire, and *one* sat upon each of them. [4]And they were all filled with the Holy Spirit and began to speak with other tongues, as the Spirit gave them utterance.

FEAST OF TRUMPETS

Also called Rosh Hashana, Trumpets is a time of spiritual awakening. It is the first of the three fall appointments, which collectively point to the return of Yeshua. Trumpets points to the "caught up" (see Glossary), the Day of Atonement points to Yeshua's second coming, and Tabernacles points to the Millennium. The three fall appointments occur during the month of Tishri, the 7th month, on the biblical calendar, which corresponds to the September-October period on the Gregorian calendar.

In the month prior to Trumpets, which takes place on Tishri 1-2, and right up to the Day of Atonement, Tishri 10, shofars are blown each day to alert the Jewish people that Atonement is coming soon. One of the main purposes of Trumpets is to get the people ready, to prepare them, for the Day of Atonement which occurs 10 days later. For believers in Yeshua, these shofars are the warning that our Atonement, Yeshua, is coming soon. Similarly, the "caught-up" (rapture) itself is the alert that He will be returning soon.

Leviticus 23:23-24 describes Trumpets: [23]Then the LORD spoke to Moses, saying, [24]"Speak to the children of Israel, saying: 'In the seventh month, on the first *day* of the month, you shall have a sabbath-*rest*, a memorial of blowing of trumpets, a holy convocation.

The trumpet, or shofar, had been blown on many important occasions in the past; such as, giving of the Torah, times of victories, new kings, others. However, it is important to examine Bible passages that show when it will be blown in the future. These future occasions are associated with the "caught up" (rapture).

1 Thessalonians 4:16-17 states: [16]For the Lord Himself will descend from heaven with a shout, with the voice of an archangel, and with the *trumpet* of God. And the dead in Christ will rise first. [17]Then we who are alive *and* remain shall be *caught up* together with them in the clouds to meet the Lord in the air. (emphasis added)

1 Corinthians 51-52 states: [51]Behold, I tell you a mystery: We shall not all sleep, but we shall all be changed—[52]in a moment, in the twinkling of an eye, at the last *trumpet*. For the *trumpet will sound*, and the dead will be raised incorruptible, and we shall be changed. (emphasis added)

These are the two basic passages that nearly all Bible scholars agree point to the rapture. They describe a movement of people from earth to heaven, and while neither says "heaven" specifically, other passages make it clear that this is the case (e.g., John 14:2-3). The above passages associate the rapture with the sounding of the shofar. There are, of course, times when the shofar is sounded in other passages not relating to the rapture, but the context of the Feast of Trumpets is getting ready for the Day of Atonement which follows – just as the rapture warns that the second coming is near.

For both the Pre-tribulation and Pre-wrath (Glossary) rapture scenarios, raptured believers will spend time in heaven (John 14:2-3) before returning with Yeshua at His second coming. If the rapture is Pre-trib, they will spend seven or more years in heaven; and if the rapture is Pre-wrath, they will spend about one and a half years in heaven. Believers must be in heaven for some period of time for the marriage of Yeshua and His bride (Revelation 19:7) and for other events in Revelation 19. A Post-tribulation rapture is not considered possible because, among other reasons, it is not supported by John 14:2-3 and Revelation 19.

DAY OF ATONEMENT (Yom Kippur)

Whereas Yahweh's other appointments emphasize joy and

97

thankfulness, Tishri 10, the Day of Atonement, is a solemn day – a day of yielding to Yahweh so that we may live face to face in His presence. Leviticus 23:26-28 states:

> 26And the LORD spoke to Moses, saying: 27"Also the tenth *day* of this seventh month *shall be* the Day of Atonement. It shall be a holy convocation for you; you shall afflict your souls, and offer an offering made by fire to the LORD. 28And you shall do no work on that same day, for it *is* the Day of Atonement, to make atonement for you before the LORD your God.

It was the day when the sins of the Israel nation were covered once a year by the high priest, who entered the Holy of Holies in the temple to offer blood to atone for the sins of the people. Hebrews 9:7-8 states:

> . . . the high priest *went* alone once a year, not without blood, which he offered for himself and *for* the people's sins *committed* in ignorance; 8the Holy Spirit indicating this, that the way into the Holiest of All was not yet made manifest while the first tabernacle was still standing.

However, believers in Yeshua know that we have, upon repentance, forgiveness of sin for eternity because of His perfect, one-time sacrifice. Hebrews 9:11-12, 28 states:

> 11But Christ came *as* High Priest of the good things to come, with the greater and more perfect tabernacle not made with hands, that is, not of this creation. 12Not with the blood of goats and calves, but with His own blood He entered the Most Holy Place once for all, having obtained eternal redemption. . . 28 Christ was offered once to bear the sins of many. *To those who eagerly wait for Him He will appear a second time*, apart from sin, for salvation. (emphasis added)

Today, believers eagerly wait for His return, and the Day of Atonement points to this second coming. Except for Messianic

Jewish believers, Israel does not at this time realize that Yeshua is their Messiah, but when He physically returns to the Mount of Olives (Zechariah 12:4) and they see Him, they will know that He is indeed their long-awaited Messiah. Romans 11:26-27 and Zechariah 12:10 state:

> [26]And so all Israel will be saved, as it is written:
> *"The Deliverer will come out of Zion,*
> *And He will turn away ungodliness from Jacob;*
> [27]*For this is My covenant with them, When I take away*
> *their sins."*

> Zechariah 12: [10]"And I will pour on the house of David and on the inhabitants of Jerusalem the Spirit of grace and supplication; then they will look on Me whom they pierced. Yes, they will mourn for Him as one mourns for *his* only *son,* and grieve for Him as one grieves for a firstborn.

Yeshua's second coming is Israel's real Day of Atonement.

FEAST OF TABERNACLES

Tabernacles is a time of great joy and celebration, and is observed during Tishri 15-22, which falls in September-October on the Gregorian calendar. It reminds us of Yahweh's sovereignty and majesty, and it is a time of thanking Him for His provision. Leviticus 23 states:

> [33]Then the LORD spoke to Moses, saying, [34]"Speak to the children of Israel, saying: 'The fifteenth day of this seventh month *shall be* the Feast of Tabernacles *for* seven days to the LORD. [35]On the first day *there shall be* a holy convocation. You shall do no customary work *on it.* . . . [39]'Also on the fifteenth day of the seventh month, when you have gathered in the fruit of the land, you shall keep the feast of the LORD *for* seven days; on the first day *there shall be* a sabbath-*rest,* and on the eighth day a sabbath-*rest.* [40]And you shall take for your-

selves on the first day the fruit of beautiful trees, branches of palm trees, the boughs of leafy trees, and willows of the brook; and you shall rejoice before the LORD your God for seven days. [41] You shall keep it as a feast to the LORD for seven days in the year. *It shall be* a statute forever in your generations.

Tabernacles reminds the Israelites of Yahweh's provision for 40 years of wandering in the wilderness. It is the final wheat harvest for the year, reminding us of the great harvest that Yeshua will gather at His second coming. Zechariah 14:16 and Micah 4:1-2 capture the scene very well:

[16] And it shall come to pass *that* everyone who is left of all the nations which came against Jerusalem shall go up from year to year to worship the King, the LORD of hosts, and to keep the Feast of Tabernacles.

[1] Now it shall come to pass in the latter days *That* the mountain of the LORD'S house
Shall be established on the top of the mountains, And shall be exalted above the hills;
And peoples shall flow to it. Many nations shall come and say,
"Come, and let us go up to the mountain of the LORD, To the house of the God of Jacob;
He will teach us His ways, And we shall walk in His paths."
For out of Zion the law shall go forth, And the word of the LORD from Jerusalem.

There can be little doubt that this final appointment does indeed point to the Millennial reign of Yeshua, which is ushered in by His second coming.

WAS CHRISTMAS
THE TIME OF YESHUA'S BIRTH?

The church realizes that Christmas, with its pagan traditions, is not really Yeshua's Birthday. December 25th was celebrated in ancient times as the birthday of the *SUN* god, Mithras, well before Yeshua was born. Christmas was not celebrated by the church until the 4th century – Christians did not honor Christmas for the first 300 years. In order to win gentile converts to the Christian faith, the Holy Roman Catholic Church adopted this ancient pagan winter festival, and renamed it Christ-Mass.

The Essential Catholic Handbook gives an almost humorous view of Christmas were it not so pathetic: "Many of the customs that have grown over the centuries to celebrate Christmas had their origin in the pagan celebration of the beginning of winter but have been 'christened' with a religious significance." (2) So, is it really true that just by using the magic "christening" wand we can give pagan rites "religious significance"? Any person or institution that believes this is in for quite a surprise. Yahweh has warned repeatedly in the Bible that harboring paganism will bring His wrath.

With the Protestant Reformation in the 1500s, any celebrations not specifically in the Bible became illegal. The first successful European settlers in the New World were Puritans, the pilgrims of Plymouth Colony. These colonists made Christmas celebrations illegal in America through the Decree of 1657. Pastor George Udvary writes: "Then on May 11, 1659, in Massachusetts, the colonial legislature passed its anti-holiday law, reading, 'Whosoever shall be found observing any such day as Christmas . . . shall pay for every offense five shillings.'"*(3)*

The 1st century Christians did not celebrate Christmas, but they did celebrate the Sabbath and Leviticus 23 festivals. It is wonderful to celebrate Yeshua's birthday, but it seems that the day of celebration should be reasonably close to His actual birth date, and certainly not on some pagan god's birth date.

The church in general simply accepts the pagan origins of Christmas and moves on with the celebrations – it is just "business as usual". For example, the following paragraph was taken from a paper on Christmas that was recently distributed for information purposes in an adult Sunday school class at the United Evangelical Free Church, Klamath Falls, Oregon:

"Christmas customs are an evolution from times that long antedated Christmas. In the beginning many of earth's inhabitants were sun worshippers because their lives depended on the sun, so many feasts were held to honor it. In Egypt and Persia, for example, the sun-gods were worshipped with elaborate ceremonies at the season of the winter solstice (Encyclopedia Britannica). Some examples of customs: holly berries were sacred to the sun god (and decorate the holly wreath of today) and the yule log derives from a pagan symbol of the sun".

Although Mithraism was discussed in Chapter 3, there is a close relationship of Christmas to this mystery religion. Yahweh's Restoration Ministry described it in this way: "Historians do not hide the fact that Christmas was an invention of the Roman church, designed to compete with the heathen Roman feast of Saturnalia in honor of the sun deity Mithras. Mithras bore remarkable similarity to the Biblical Messiah. The Mithraic feast, like Christmas, was celebrated to commemorate his birth . . . His birth on December 25 was witnessed by shepherds. After many deeds he held a last supper with his disciples and returned to heaven. At the end of the world he will come again to judge mankind . . . No wonder the early Christians were disturbed by a deity who bore so close a resemblance to their own . . . When the Protestant movement attempted to rid itself of the excesses and sins of Roman Catholicism, there also came an opposition to Christmas that almost obliterated it entirely in England. . . . In America, strong religious antagonism to the feast of Christmas lasted from 1620 to 1750—130 years!" *(4)*

YESHUA'S BIRTH WAS
AROUND THE TIME OF TABERNACLES

The Bible does not give the date of Yeshua's birth; however, close examination of the Scriptures allows us to conclude that He was born some time in the autumn of the year. There is convincing evidence that His birth was about the time of the Feast of Tabernacles, which occurs in the early autumn. Also, shepherds would not have been tending their sheep in late December, because it was winter and too cold. It is ironic that Christian churches will refer to Luke Chapter 1 as the story of how Yeshua was born on December 25th, and yet reading this chapter carefully shows that He was really born around the time of Tabernacles.

In Luke Chapter 1, the births of both John the Baptist and Yeshua are foretold. The angel Gabriel visited Zechariah, who was a priest, during the priestly division of Abijah (v. 5), which was the 8th of 24 divisions during a 12 month year (1 Chronicles 24:7-10). Gabriel announced to Zechariah that his wife Elizabeth was pregnant with John. Since each priestly division served two weeks in the temple, Zechariah's division would be serving during weeks 15 and 16 after the start of the year.

The new year on the biblical calendar begins with the new moon nearest to the spring equinox, which is March 20th. Fifteen weeks after March 20th brings us to early July as the time when Gabriel told Zechariah that Elizabeth would bear a son whose name was to be John. Now, six months into her pregnancy, early January, Gabriel also informed Mary that she was pregnant and would give birth to Yeshua (Luke 1:26-33). Counting nine months from early January gives September-October as the probable time of Yeshua's birth, which is about the time of the Feast of Tabernacles.

THROUGH YAHWEH'S EYES

Let's pause and try to see this situation through His eyes. Even though not required, Christians want to honor Yeshua's birth, which seems a fine thing to do. But – why did the church choose December 25th, which is the birthday of the ancient sun god Mithras (also known as Tammuz) who is straight out of paganism? The church has elected to not study Luke 1, which gives biblical evidence as to when He was actually born. Even so, at least it could have chosen any date but one connected to a pagan god. As mentioned in Chapter 3, this is a perfect illustration of blending a biblical event (Yeshua's birthday) with a pagan event (December 25th was Mithras/Tammuz'birthday).

In summary, the church has not received the joy of celebrating Yahweh's appointments in Leviticus 23 because it is blind to spiritual applications of the Hebrew Scriptures/Torah. The church has been missing wonderful opportunities to commemorate what Yeshua did for us at His first coming, and what He will do for us when He returns. Sadly, it is the individual Christian who suffers from a church gone astray.

Jeremiah 10:3-4: [3]For the customs of the peoples *are* futile; For *one* cuts a tree from the forest, The work of the hands of the workman, with the ax. [4]They decorate it with silver and gold; They fasten it with nails and hammers So that it will not topple.
(Could this be a Christmas tree?)

Ezekiel 8:12-14: [12]Then He said to me, "Son of man, have you seen what the elders of the house of Israel do in the dark, every man in the room of his idols? For they say, 'The LORD does not see us, the LORD has forsaken the land.'" [13]And He said to me, "Turn again, *and* you will see greater abominations that they are doing." [14]So He brought me to the door of the north gate of the LORD'S house; and to my dismay, women were sitting there weeping for *TAMMUZ* (emphasis added).

7. THE RESTORATION OF ISRAEL – PHASE I

⸺⬥⬥⬥⸺

The negative forces acting to separate Judaism and Christianity were discussed in Chapters 2 and 3, and the consequences of this separation have been explored in Chapters 4, 5, and 6. The positive forces moving to heal the 1900 years of separation are discussed here and in the next chapter. It will be seen that Yahweh is in the process of restoring Israel, as numerous prophecies have already been fulfilled and many others are being fulfilled.

The complete restoration of Israel will be an amazing and wondrous work of Yahweh. Fulfilled prophecies are so awesome that any unbeliever who will just spend one hour objectively reviewing them might come to the realization that Yahweh is indeed who He says He is: the creator and sustainer of everything we see.

Many believe that Christianity replaced Israel in Yahweh's plan (known as replacement theology), and that therefore the "restoration of Israel" is simply not something of concern. Nothing could be further from the truth – much of the Bible speaks to His sovereign plan to provide complete restoration of Israel. To believe that Israel will not be restored means that around a third of the Bible's passages are being ignored and thrown out. Israel's restoration is one of the most discussed topics in it – why believe in the Bible at all if nearly one third is to be simply disregarded?

Here is what the Bible says will happen if Israel is not restored. In Jeremiah Chapter 31, Yahweh gives the New Covenant describing Yeshua's coming, and verses 31:35-36 speak specifically about Israel's future restoration:

> 35Thus says the LORD, Who gives the sun for a light by day,
> The ordinances of the moon and the stars for a light by night,
> Who disturbs the sea, And its waves roar (The LORD of hosts
>   *is* His name):
> 36"If those ordinances depart From before Me, says the LORD,
> *Then* the seed of Israel shall also cease From being a nation
>   before Me forever."

Thus, only if this planet ceased to exist because the sun, moon, stars and sea disappeared, would the nation of Israel cease to exist. Acts Chapter 1, among other passages, also makes it abundantly clear that the kingdom will be restored to Israel: 6Therefore, when they had come together, they asked Him, saying, "Lord, will You at this time restore the kingdom to Israel?" 7And He said to them, "It is not for you to know times or seasons which the Father has put in His own authority."

Yeshua acknowledges that the kingdom will be restored to Israel, but that only the *time* of this restoration is being held secret by Yahweh. Another important passage heralding

Israel's longevity is Romans 11:25-27:

> 25For I do not desire, brethren, that you should be ignorant of
>   this mystery, lest you should be wise in your own opinion,
>   that blindness in part has happened to Israel until the full-
>   ness of the Gentiles has come in. 26And so all Israel will
>   be saved, as it is written:
> *"The Deliverer will come out of Zion, And He will turn*
>   *away ungodliness from Jacob;*
> 27*For this is My covenant with them, When I take away*
>   *their sins."*

Can there be any doubt that the clause *"all Israel will be saved"* means other than she will be restored?

With the preceding as an overview of Israel's future significance, it is important to note that numerous Christians today have been led away from a true biblical understanding of where Israel fits into the Bible. The misguided thinking that the church has replaced Israel, replacement theology, is not only far from what the Bible really says, but it also adds fuel to the continuing growth of anti-Semitism. As discussed in preceding chapters, anti-Semitism is once again becoming a significant worldwide issue. Reports coming out of Europe suggest it is approaching the level of Nazi Germany before WW II. Christians everywhere need to thoroughly understand exactly what the Bible says about Israel's future, and not base their understanding on the lies and deception of the early church fathers and those after them who are responsible for continuing to cover up the truth.

ISRAEL'S RESTORATION –
IN PROCESS OF BEING FULFILLED

To begin, we first should review a few of the many *literally* fulfilled prophecies that deal with Israel. Recalling these will remind us not only of Yahweh's awesome power, but also of the certain knowledge that the rest of His plan for Israel will be fulfilled exactly as written.

In Genesis 15:12-14 (written about 1900 BC) Yahweh said that Israel would be enslaved by a foreign country for 400 years: [12]Now when the sun was going down, a deep sleep fell upon Abram; and behold, horror *and* great darkness fell upon him. [13]Then He said to Abram: "Know certainly that your descendants will be strangers in a land *that is* not theirs, and will serve them, and they will afflict them four hundred years. [14]And also the nation whom they serve I will judge.

This prophecy was fulfilled around 1500 BC in Exodus 12:40: Now the time that the children of Israel dwelt in Egypt was four hundred and thirty years.

In Genesis 12:1-3 (written about 1900 BC) Yahweh said that Abraham would become a great nation and through him all people will be blessed: [1]Now the LORD had said to Abram: "Get out of your country; From your family and from your father's house, To a land that I will show you. [2] I will make you a great nation; I will bless you and make your name great;

And you shall be a blessing. 3 I will bless those who bless you, And I will curse him who curses you; And in you all the families of the earth shall be blessed."

This prophecy has been and continues to be fulfilled. Israel became a great nation, and Yeshua came to be a blessing to all those in the world who would come to Him. There are also many nations from ancient times to the present that have been destroyed because they "cursed" Israel beyond what Yahweh allowed, as mentioned at the end of Chapter 3. The magazine, Zion's Fire, also provides perspective on this: "Obviously, history verifies the nation's (Israel's) great sufferings over the years. However, those sufferings have been permitted by God for the chastening of His people. But it is a proven fact that those who sought to go beyond that – to actually wipe Israel off the face of the earth – have tasted the fury of God's wrath." *(1)*

In Deuteronomy 28:37 (written about 1420 BC) Yahweh said that, because of Israel's disobedience, she would become a thing of horror and an object of scorn: [37]And you shall become an astonishment, a proverb, and a byword among all nations where the LORD will drive you.

This has been fulfilled through history, and in more recent times, through the Russian pogroms and Nazi Holocaust. Israel's disobedience has been punished exactly as Yahweh said it would be. In Deuteronomy 28:64-67 (written about 1420 BC) Yahweh said the Israel would be scattered and terrorized:

> [64]"Then the LORD will scatter you among all peoples, from one end of the earth to the other, and there you shall serve other gods, which neither you nor your fathers have known—wood and stone. [65]And among those nations you shall find no rest, nor shall the sole of your foot have a resting place; but there the LORD will give you a trembling heart, failing eyes, and anguish of soul. [66]Your life shall hang in doubt before you; you *shall fear day and night*, and have no assurance of life. [67]In the morning you shall say, 'Oh, that it were evening!' And at evening you shall say, 'Oh, that it were morning!' because of the *fear which terrifies your heart*, and because of the sight which your eyes see. (emphasis added)

Israel has been scattered to nations around the world. She has been terrorized (in other Bible versions, "terror" is used instead of "fear") ever since becoming a nation in 1948. Repeated terror attacks by the surrounding Arab countries continue to this day in a continuing effort to destroy her. Israel is most certainly not finding rest in other nations.

Psalm 83:4-8 predicted the ongoing Arab attacks to destroy Israel:

> [4]They have said, "Come, and let us cut them off from *being* a nation,
>
> That the name of Israel may be remembered no more." [5] they have consulted together with one consent; They
>
> Form a confederacy against You: the tents of Edom and the Ishmaelites;
>
> Moab and the Hagrites; Gebal, Ammon, and Amalek; Philistia with the inhabitants of Tyre;
>
> [8]Assyria also has joined with them; They have helped the children of Lot.

The countries named in these verses are the forefathers of the Arab nations surrounding Israel today. The Arabs' plan, regardless of whatever peace treaty is signed in the future, is the destruction of Israel. Their strategy has always been, and remains, to sign any contract or treaty that will give them time to prepare for another attempt to drive Israel into the sea. Anti-Semitism first started with the Arabs' forefathers, Ishmael and Esau, and has been accelerated by the church over the last 19 centuries. See Appendix A for discussion of Ishmael, Esau, and their descendants.

Isaiah 44:28 (written about 740 BC) predicted that King Cyrus of Persia would authorize the rebuilding of Jerusalem and the temple that had been destroyed by the Babylonians: [28]Who says of Cyrus, '*He is* My shepherd, And he shall perform all My pleasure, Saying to Jerusalem, "You shall be built," And to the temple, "Your foundation shall be laid".

This prophecy was fulfilled in Ezra 5:1-2 (about 580 BC, 160 years later) when Cyrus authorized the rebuilding of Jerusalem and the temple:

> ¹Now in the first year of Cyrus king of Persia, that the word of the LORD by the mouth of Jeremiah might be fulfilled, the LORD stirred up the spirit of Cyrus king of Persia, so that he made a proclamation throughout all his kingdom, and also *put it* in writing, saying, Thus says Cyrus king of Persia: All the kingdoms of the earth the LORD God of heaven has given me. And He has commanded me to build Him a house at Jerusalem which *is* in Judah.

In Isaiah 66:8 (written about 740 BC), the Bible predicts that a nation will be created in a day:

> ⁸Who has heard such a thing? Who has seen such things?
> Shall the earth be made to give birth in one day? *Or* shall a
>   nation be born at once?
> For as soon as Zion was in labor, She gave birth to her children.

Israel was reborn as a nation in one day in 1948, after it had been totally conquered and its people scattered nearly 19 centuries earlier. Even though the United Nations today spends nearly half of its time condemning Israel for defending itself from Arab terrorism, Yahweh saw to it that this organization would cause Israel to be reborn.

Isaiah Chapters 52 and 53 (written about 740 BC) contain numerous prophecies about the Messiah of Israel, Yeshua, which specifically point to events concerning His death and suffering on the tree. All were *literally* fulfilled in the New Testament.

In Zechariah 12:2-3 (written about 530 BC), Yahweh said that Jerusalem would become such a difficult problem that the nations would go to war over her: ²"Behold, I will make Jerusalem a cup of drunkenness to all the surrounding peoples, when they lay siege against Judah and Jerusalem. ³And it shall happen in that day that I will make Jerusalem a very heavy stone for all peoples; all who would heave it away will surely be cut in pieces, though all nations of the earth are gathered against it.

This prophecy has already been fulfilled since Israel was reborn in 1948, and continues to be fulfilled today. Jerusalem – seemingly a relatively unimportant city in terms of population, location, commerce and other things – has the undivided attention of the world as the nations continue to stumble over her. "In that day" points to the final battle of Armageddon at the end of the tribulation period when Yeshua returns to save Israel from all the nations attacking her. The "Jerusalem clock" is ticking and the present time seems to be about 11:55 pm. From now on the world's eyes should be focused on this clock, because at midnight the end of this age arrives as Yeshua returns to Jerusalem.

In Ezekiel 36:8-9 (written about 580 BC), Yahweh said that Israel will again produce much fruit:

> [8]But you, O mountains of Israel, you shall shoot forth your branches and yield your fruit to My people Israel, for they are about to come. [9]For indeed I *am* for you, and I will turn to you, and you shall be tilled and sown.

Modern day Israel is again a land flowing with "milk and honey" since her people have returned. She now is producing so much fruit that she has become one of the world's leading exporters.

In Isaiah 43:5-6 (written about 700 BC), Yahweh predicted that He would regather His people from the east, the west, the north and the south:

> [5]Fear not, for I *am* with you; I will bring your descendants
>   from the east,
> And gather you from the west; [6] I will say to the north, 'Give
>   them up!'
> And to the south, 'Do not keep them back!' Bring My sons
>   from afar,
> And My daughters from the ends of the earth—

Not only does Yahweh predict the future re-gathering of His people, but He also gives the ***order*** of their return: First, Jewish people returned from Arab nations to the *east*, then they returned from Europe and the U.S. in the *west*, then from Russia in the *north*, and finally from Ethiopia in the *south*. This pertains to the initial immigrations during the past 50-60 years. Immigrants continue to return from all areas of the world.

PROPHECIES CONCERNING ISRAEL'S FUTURE RESTORATION

Having looked at a few of the many fulfilled prophecies concerning Israel, let us now look at prophecies showing her continuing and then final restoration.

In Isaiah 11:11-12 (written about 700 BC), Yahweh said that He would regather Israel's people a *second* time from the nations where they had been scattered: [11]It shall come to pass in that day *That* the Lord shall set His hand again the second time To recover the remnant of His people who are left, From Assyria and Egypt, From Pathros and Cush, From Elam and Shinar, From Hamath and the islands of the sea. [12] He will set up a banner for the nations, And will assemble the outcasts of Israel, And gather together the dispersed of Judah From the four corners of the earth.

Isaiah 49:22 (written about 700 BC) predicts that gentiles will help bring Jewish people back to the land: [22]Thus says the Lord GOD: "Behold, I will lift My hand in an oath to the nations, And set up My standard for the peoples; They shall bring your sons in *their* arms, And your daughters shall be carried on *their* shoulders;

In Jeremiah 16:15 (written about 600 BC), the future dispersion and re-gathering of Israel is predicted: [15]but, 'The LORD lives who brought up the children of Israel from the land of the north and from all the lands where He had driven them.' For I will bring them back into their land which I gave to their fathers.

In 70 AD the people of Israel were scattered around the world. Many returned during the following decades, only to be dispersed again when the Romans destroyed Jerusalem in 135. But now we have seen the re-gathering of millions of Jewish people to the land of Israel, and it continues.

Jeremiah 30:10-11 (written about 600 BC) also predicts the re-gathering of Israel and the final destruction of other nations: [10]'Therefore do not fear, O My servant Jacob,' says the LORD, 'Nor be dismayed, O Israel; For behold, I will save you from afar, And your seed from the land of their captivity.

> Jacob shall return, have rest and be quiet, And no one shall make *him* afraid. ¹¹For I *am* with you,' says the LORD, 'to save you; Though I make a full end of all nations where I have scattered you,
>
> Yet I will not make a complete end of you. But I will correct you in justice,

Ezekiel 36:24-28 (written about 580 BC) predicts that first Israel will receive physical restoration and finally spiritual restoration: ²⁴For I will take you from among the nations, gather you out of all countries, and bring you into your own land. ²⁵Then I will sprinkle clean water on you, and you shall be clean; I will cleanse you from all your filthiness and from all your idols. ²⁶I will give you a new heart and put a new spirit within you; I will take the heart of stone out of your flesh and give you a heart of flesh. ²⁷I will put My Spirit within you and cause you to walk in My statutes, and you will keep My judgments and do *them.* ²⁸Then you shall dwell in the land that I gave to your fathers; you shall be My people, and I will be your God.

There are numerous other prophecies in the Hebrew Scriptures that predict Israel's restoration, but it would require a separate book to discuss them. However, the above examples should suffice to demonstrate that Yahweh is restoring Israel, and this restoration will be complete physically and spiritually. It is unfortunate that Israel today is extremely secular, and is definitely not a Yahweh-fearing nation. However, the bright side of this is that when He does finally restore her, the other nations of the world will be awestruck, and they will then know that Yahweh is indeed the one and only God of the universe.

Up to this point, the first part of Yahweh's restoration plan for Israel has been discussed, which involved the re-gathering of the Jewish people in the land of Israel. However, a second part of His restoration plan revolves around the ten northern tribes who seceded from Judah and Benjamin in 931 BC, thus dividing Israel into two separate nations. The next chapter addresses this second part.

8. THE RESTORATION of ISRAEL – PHASE II

Behold, how good and how pleasant *it is f*or brethren to dwell together in unity! (Psalm 133:1)

The Bible says that the complete restoration of Israel will include more than just restoring the Jewish people to Israel. There is a second part of Yahweh's plan that needs to be examined for an understanding of His complete restoration. It is of fundamental importance to Yahweh that the *whole* of Israel be restored to the land physically and spiritually.

DIVISION OF ISRAEL INTO TWO SEPARATE NATIONS

Numerous passages in the Hebrew Scriptures/Torah refer to the division of Israel in 931 BC, after Solomon's reign, into two separate nations: Ephraim/Northern Kingdom of Israel and Southern Kingdom of Judah (the "Jews"). Recall that the term "Jews", or "men of Judah", first appears in the Bible in II Kings 16:6. The northern kingdom also became known as "Ephraim" because it was the dominant tribe, and many of the leaders in the Northern Kingdom were Ephraimites. The split of Israel into the two nations was not just a temporary one. It was permanent, and Yahweh from this point on treated them as separate and distinct nations.

The Ephraimites were loyal to Israel's first king, Saul. They never attained the same relationship with David, the successor king, who was from Judah. Years later Jeroboam, an Ephraimite, led the northern kingdom to become independent of Judah, and the division of Israel into Israel/Ephraim and Judah/Jews resulted. From that time on, Yahweh through the prophets used the term Israel/Ephraim to refer to the northern kingdom, which continued to be led and dominated by Ephraimites.

A series of wars between the two houses took place during the several centuries after the split. Later, Ephraim/Northern Kingdom of Israel was subsequently taken captive by the Assyrians in 722 BC, and the people were then removed to Assyria (northeast of present-day Israel). Yahweh allowed this Assyrian captivity because of Israel/Ephraim's gross idolatry. As the captive population was removed from the land of Israel, captives from other parts of the Assyrian empire were resettled in their place. Over the centuries, after the captivity, descendants of the ten tribes making up Ephraim were scattered to other nations of the world, including to the southern kingdom of Judah. The Bible makes clear that they, in addition to the Jewish people, will be re-gathered and restored to the land of Israel.

THE RETURN OF JUDAH (JEWS)
AND EPHRAIM (ISRAEL) TO THE LAND

Isaiah 11:10-12, a passage mentioned earlier, expresses clearly that Judah and Ephraim are *both* returning to the land of Israel:

> 11 It shall come to pass in that day *That* the Lord shall set His hand again the second time
> To recover the remnant of His people who are left, From Assyria and Egypt,
> From Pathros and Cush, From Elam and Shinar, From Hamath and the islands of the sea.
> 12 He will set up *a banner* for the nations, And will *assemble the outcasts of Israel*,

> And ***gather together the dispersed of Judah*** From the four
> corners of the earth.
> [13]Also the envy of Ephraim shall depart, And the adversaries
> of Judah shall be cut off;
> Ephraim shall not envy Judah, And Judah shall not harass
> Ephraim. (emphasis added)

At some future time, both Judah and Ephraim will have been
gathered to the land of Israel by Yahweh, who will use a ***"banner"***,
Yeshua, to accomplish this. The countries listed along with "the
islands of the sea" in v.11 refers to all His people who are spread
around the world; v.12 shows the gathering of the dispersed Jews
(Judah) and the gathering of Israel/Ephraim; and v.13 refers to that
future time when Judah and Ephraim are reunited.

Hosea 1:11 also states that Judah and Ephraim will be restored:
Then the children of Judah and the children of Israel (Ephraim) shall be gathered
together, And appoint for themselves one head; And they shall come up out of the
land, For great *will be* the day of Jezreel!

Zechariah 10:6-7 reconfirms this: [6]"I will strengthen the house of
Judah, And I will save the house of Joseph. I will bring them back, Because I
have mercy on them. They shall be as though I had not cast them aside; For I *am*
the LORD their God, And I will hear them. T*hose of* Ephraim shall be like a
mighty man, And their heart shall rejoice as if with wine. Yes, their children shall
see *it* and be glad; Their heart shall rejoice in the LORD.

The return of Judah/Jews to Israel started early in the 20th
century, and then accelerated in the 2nd half of the century. Large
numbers of Jewish people were allowed to leave the Soviet Union
starting in the early 1990s, and by 2000 around 1,000,000 Jews had
returned to Israel. Large influxes from other countries also took
place during the 1990s.

Notice in Isaiah 11:12 that Yahweh also "will gather the
outcasts of Israel". These are the descendants of Israel/Ephraim
who were scattered around the world after the Assyrian captivity.
These people are still awaiting His call for their return to the land.
In Isaiah 11:13 it should also be noted that after Israel/Ephraim and
Judah/Jews are reunited in the land the envy and harassment
between them will cease. The discussion in this chapter will elabo-

rate on this reunion, which is fulfillment of prophecies in Ezekiel 37.

THE COMING REUNION OF JUDAH/JEWS AND ISRAEL/EPHRAIM

The amazing prophecies in Ezekiel 37 describe Yahweh's plan for reuniting Israel/Ephraim and Judah. Verses 15-28 state:

> [15]The word of the LORD came to me: [16]"Son of man, take a stick of wood and write on it, 'Belonging to Judah and the Israelites associated with him.' Then take another stick of wood, and write on it, 'Ephraim's stick, belonging to Joseph and all the house of Israel associated with him.' [17]Join them together into one stick so that they will become one in your hand.
>
> [18]"When your countrymen ask you, 'Won't you tell us what you mean by this?' [19]say to them, 'This is what the Sovereign LORD says: *I am going to take the stick of Joseph—which is in Ephraim's hand—and of the Israelite tribes associated with him, and join it to Judah's stick, making them a single stick of wood, and they will become one in my hand.'* [20]Hold before their eyes the sticks you have written on [21]and say to them, 'This is what the Sovereign LORD says: I will take the Israelites out of the nations where they have gone. I will gather them from all around and bring them back into their own land. [22]*I will make them one nation in the land, on the mountains of Israel. There will be one king over all of them and they will never again be two nations or be divided into two kingdoms.* [23]*They will no longer defile themselves with their idols and vile images or with any of their offenses, for I will save them from all their sinful backsliding,* and I will cleanse them. They will be my people, and I will be their God.
>
> [24]"'My servant David will be king over them, and they will all have one shepherd. They will follow my laws and be careful to keep my decrees. [25]They will live in the land I gave

to my servant Jacob, the land where your fathers lived. They
and their children and their children's children will live there
forever, and David my servant will be their prince forever. [26]I
will make a covenant of peace with them; it will be an everlast-
ing covenant. I will establish them and increase their numbers,
and I will put my sanctuary among them forever. [27]*My
dwelling place will be with them; I will be their God, and they
will be my people.* [28]*Then the nations will know that I the
LORD make Israel holy, when my sanctuary is among them
forever.'"* (emphasis added)

Some may say that this reunion has already occurred, but this is
incorrect for at least two good reasons: 1. Later in this chapter it
will be seen that, while many in the northern kingdom of Ephraim
did rejoin Judah's kingdom after the Assyrian captivity, numerous
others were scattered around the world. 2. If their reunion had
already occurred, the nations would know that the "LORD makes
Israel holy" (v.28), and this most *definitely has not occurred.*
Likewise, Yahweh's *sanctuary is clearly not among them now.*

BIBLICAL IDENTIFICATION
OF ISRAEL/EPHRAIM'S DESCENDANTS

The issue of who Ephraim's descendants are has been the
subject of books and articles (1,2,3), and has become known as the
two houses theory, which addresses various future aspects of the
house of Israel/Ephraim and the house of Judah/Jews after the division into the two houses. This issue is a very sensitive one for a
number of reasons; accordingly, care has been taken to discuss it
only in terms of what the Bible clearly says about it.

In about 1650 BC, when Jacob blessed Ephraim (son of
Joseph), he prophesied that Ephraim would become the father of
many gentile nations. Genesis 48:17-19 states:

[17]Now when Joseph saw that his father laid his right hand
on the head of Ephraim, it displeased him; so he took hold of
his father's hand to remove it from Ephraim's head to

Manasseh's head. [18]And Joseph said to his father, "Not so, my father, for this *one is* the firstborn; put your right hand on his head."

[19]But his father refused and said, "I know, my son, I know. He also shall become a people, and he also shall be great; but truly his younger brother shall be greater than he, and ***his descendants shall become a multitude of nations.***" (emphasis added)

Ephraim's descendants became a *multitude of nations*. Even before Jacob gave Ephraim the blessing, Genesis 35:11 had previously stated that nations would descend from Jacob:

[9]Then God appeared to Jacob again, when he came from Padan Aram, and blessed him. [10]And God said to him, "Your name *is* Jacob; your name shall not be called Jacob anymore, but Israel shall be your name." So He called his name Israel. [11]Also God said to him: "I *am* God Almighty. Be fruitful and multiply; *a nation and a company of nations shall proceed from you,* and kings shall come from your body. (emphasis added)

"A nation" likely refers to the southern kingdom of Judah, and it follows that "a company of nations" refers to the descendants of Israel/Ephraim.

The prophet Hosea (about 750 BC) was the prophet Yahweh used to communicate with Ephraim, the Northern House of Israel. Yahweh became very displeased with Ephraim's descendants because of their extreme disobedience. At one point, He referred to the Israelites (Ephraim) as not His people. Hosea 1:9 states: For you *are* not My people, and I will not be your *God.*

Yahweh goes on to indicate the punishments He is applying to Israel/Ephraim in Hosea 2 because of her extreme disobedience, for as Hosea 2:11-12 states:

[11]I will also cause all her mirth to cease, Her feast days, Her New Moons, Her Sabbaths—All her appointed feasts.

12"And I will destroy her vines and her fig trees, Of which she has said, 'These *are* my wages that my lovers have given me.' So I will make them a forest, And the beasts of the field shall eat them.

I will punish her For the days of the Baals to which she burned incense.

He took away Ephraim's joy of feast days (Yahweh's appointments in Leviticus 23); he took away her new moons and calendar (Yahweh's biblical calendar depends on knowing when new moons begin); and He took away the joy of the Sabbath. Ephraim/Israel became blinded to these joyous times that Yahweh had established.

IS ISRAEL/EPHRAIM SOMEHOW RELATED TO THE CHURCH?

It seems that Israel/Ephraim bears some resemblance to the church, which also has been blinded to the joy of these times. The church created its own set of holidays and events based on unbiblical pagan rites because it had rejected the Torah and refused to accept Yahweh's appointed times in Leviticus 23. It also developed a pagan calendar, based on the solar cycle and pagan gods, in place of Yahweh's biblical calendar that is based on the lunar cycle. And, the church decided that Sunday would be its day of worship because the early "church fathers" and Mithraism led it away from accepting that the 7th day Sabbath (Saturday) is Yahweh's holy day of rest – not Sunday which had pagan origins. As with Ephraim/Israel, the church takes no joy in the Sabbath, because Yahweh caused this joy ("mirth") to cease long ago as a punishment for disobedience.

Let us examine further Scripture and see if a relationship between Israel/Ephraim and the church is confirmed. Following are additional passages from Hosea which provide further insight on this issue:

Hosea 4:6 — 6My people are destroyed for lack of *knowledge*: because thou hast rejected knowledge, I will also reject thee, that thou shalt be no priest to me: seeing thou hast forgotten the law *(Torah)* of thy God, I will also forget thy children.

Hosea 4:17 — [17]Ephraim *is joined to idols*: let him alone.

Hosea 7:8 — [8]Ephraim, he hath **mixed himself among the people**; Ephraim is a cake not turned.

Hosea 8:8-10 — [8]Israel is swallowed up: **now shall they be among the Gentiles** as a vessel wherein *is* no pleasure. [9]For they are gone up to Assyria, a wild ass alone by himself: Ephraim hath hired lovers. [10]Yea, though **they have hired among the nations**, now will I gather them, (emphasis added to all verses)

In Hosea 4:6 through 8:8-10: Ephraim has forgotten the Torah — the church has forgotten the Torah; Ephraim is joined to idols – the church is joined to idols (for ex, worshiping the goddess of Easter); Ephraim is among the gentiles and the nations – the church is also among the gentiles and the nations. This is further confirming evidence of a relationship between Israel/Ephraim and the church.

Unfortunately, Israel/Ephraim became so disobedient and unfaithful that Yahweh divorced her. Jeremiah 3:6-8 states: [6]The LORD said also to me in the days of Josiah the king: "Have you seen what backsliding Israel has done? She has gone up on every high mountain and under every green tree, and there played the harlot. [7]And I said, after she had done all these *things,* 'Return to Me.' But she did not return. And her treacherous sister Judah saw it. [8]Then I saw that for all the causes for which backsliding Israel had committed adultery, I had put her away and given her a certificate of divorce . . ."

However, Yahweh in His grace said that a day would come when He will purify Israel/Ephraim and restore her. She would be changed from being "not a people" (Hosea 1:9) to sons of the living Yahweh, as the following passages from Hosea 1 and 2 state:

Hosea 1:10: "Yet the number of the children of Israel shall be as the sand of the sea, Which cannot be measured or numbered. And it shall come to pass in the place where it was said to them, 'You *are* not My people,' *There* it shall be said to them, '*You are* sons of the living God.'

Hosea 2:23: Then I will say to *those who were* not My people, 'You *are* My people!' And they shall say, '*You are* my God!'"

However, we do not need to rely only on Hosea to demonstrate the connection between Israel/Ephraiml and the church. It is now important to see the linkages between the Hosea passages and several New Testament passages.

First, consider 1 Peter 2:9-10: [9]But you *are* a chosen generation, a royal priesthood, a holy nation, His own special people, that you may proclaim the praises of Him who called you out of darkness into His marvelous light; [10]who *once were not a people but are now the people of God*, who had not obtained mercy but now have obtained mercy. (emphasis added)

In this passage, Peter is addressing gentiles, who were identified as "pilgrims" in I Peter 1:1. Peter was written around 64-65 AD, right after Nero had burned down Rome, and then blamed it on the Christians. The MacArthur Study Bible *(4)* states: "These 'pilgrims', who were probably gentiles, for the most part, possibly led to Christ by Paul and his associates, and established on Paul's teachings."

So, in the context of 1st Peter, verses 2:9-10 are addressing gentiles "who once were not a people but *are* now the people of God". Peter clearly links *at least some* Christian gentiles to Israel/Ephraim, who also "were once not a people but now are a people of God".

Now consider Romans 9:24-26: [25]As He says also in Hosea: *"I will call them My people, who were not My people, And her beloved, who was not beloved." "And it shall come to pass in the place where it was said to them, 'You are not My people,' There they shall be called sons of the living God."*

Here Paul is addressing gentiles in the city of Rome. Yahweh had proclaimed his purpose through the prophets to show that the gentiles were to become God's people (Hosea 1:10, 2:23; 1 Peter 2:10).

Thus, both Peter and Paul, in the context of addressing gentiles in the 1st century, use the very same words that Hosea used in addressing Ephraim/Israel in 580 BC. In making what seems a very small interpretative jump, it is concluded that at least some of Ephraim's descendants became believers in Yeshua and are **a portion of** the Christians who have lived through the centuries. This interpretation of the linkage between Hosea and Romans is in agreement with William Hendriksen's principles of interpretation: "Old Testament prophecies that recur in the New Testament . . . should be interpreted in light of the of the newer revelation. Thus, Hosea 2:23, in the light of Romans 9:24-26." *(5)*

Numerous Christians have descended outside of Ephraim's bloodline, so not all Christians who live today are physical descendants of Israel/Ephraim. This issue will be explored later in the chapter. While both Ephraim and Judah have been scattered to the nations, there is an important difference in the way this was done: The Jewish people (Judah) have always maintained their identity, and have been very careful and courageous in doing so, but Ephraim's identity was lost after scattering through intermarriage. His descendants assimilated in the nations' cultures, completely losing all connections to their Hebraic heritage. They became "a people who were not a people", but through Yahweh's restoration process they would become a people – His people. And, when Yahweh "restores all things" (Acts 3:21) at the end of the present age, their identities will be restored, and they will finally recognize who they really are.

From this point on, Israel/Ephraim is called Ephraim/ Christianity to emphasize that many of Ephraim's descendants are Christians. It is also important to emphasize that Ephraim/ Christianity's descendants have not displaced or replaced in any way the "Jews" who have descended from the southern house of Judah. Judah and its descendants were, and still are, Yahweh's chosen people. The Jewish people have protected the Hebrew Scriptures/Torah through the centuries, making it possible for us to have a New Testament that makes sense *only because it is based on the foundation of the Hebrew Scriptures/Torah.*

It is now appropriate to discuss Ephesians 2:13-18, because it is a parallel passage to Ezekiel 37.

> [13]But now in Christ Jesus you who once were far off have been brought near by the blood of Christ.
>
> [14]For He Himself is our peace, who has made both one, and has **broken down the middle wall of separation**, [15]having abolished in His flesh the enmity, . . . so as **to create in Himself one new man from the two**, *thus* making peace, [16]and that He might reconcile them both to God in one body through the cross, **thereby putting to death the enmity.** [17]And He came and preached peace to you who were afar off and to those who

were near. [18]For through Him we both have access by one Spirit to the Father.

This passage states that Yeshua is the means through which the "wall of separation" dividing the Jews and the Christians is "broken down", and He has created "in Himself one new man from the two". This unity has not yet been achieved, because the Jews and Christians remain as divided as ever and "enmity" (v. 16) has not been put to death. So, here we see that a future reunion of the Jews and Christians will occur.

But, Ezekiel 37 is all about the future reunion of the Jews and Israel/Ephraim. The Bible contains no passages indicating even a hint of a future reunion involving three groups. Therefore, the only possible conclusion is that Israel/Ephraim equals Christianity. In mathematical parlance:

Israel/Ephraim + Judah/Jews = Reunion (Ezekiel 37)
Christianity   + Judah/Jews = Reunion (Ephesians 2); Therefore,
Christianity = Israel/Ephraim

Yahweh's future plan in both the Hebrew Scriptures and the New Testament calls for the future reuniting of Ephraim/ Christianity and Judah/Jews. Both groups are to be reunited into one nation, never again to be divided, and He will be their one and only God forever. He never talks about reuniting three groups – Ephraim, Judah, and Christianity – but only two. This is also confirmed by Jeremiah 33:23-25:

> [23]Moreover the word of the LORD came to Jeremiah, saying, [24]"Have you not considered what these people have spoken, saying, *'The two families which the LORD has chosen*, He has also cast them off'? Thus they have despised My people, as if they should no more be a nation before them. [25]"Thus says the LORD: 'If My covenant *is* not with day and night, *and if* I have not appointed the ordinances of heaven and earth, [26]then I will cast away the *descendants of Jacob* . . . (emphasis added)

The two chosen families are the descendants of Jacob: Judah and Ephraim/Christianity. Yahweh's final restoration will not occur until Judah/Judaism accepts Yeshua as Messiah, and Ephraim/Christianity accepts the Torah (Hebrew Scriptures). Judaism has protected and believed the Torah through the centuries, but has rejected Yeshua, whereas the "Christians" through time have believed in Yeshua but have rejected the Torah, as discussed in Chapter 4.

In the present day, there is strong evidence that many Christians are starting to see the importance of living Torah-based lifestyles (see Glossary), and that many Jews are starting to see that Yeshua is indeed their Messiah. As these understandings continue to affect more and more Christians and Jews, we will be getting closer and closer to Yahweh's final restoration depicted in Ezekiel 37 and Ephesians 2.

The focus has been on Ephraim and Judah and their descendants; however, Yahweh also promised Ishmael and Esau land and many descendants, but not the divine blessing. Appendix A discusses these topics.

ROUGH ESTIMATE
OF EPHRAIMITES IN WORLD TODAY

Because Christian descendants of Ephraim are unaware of their heritage, it would be relevant to estimate how many there are. If an estimate of them were to show a relatively small population, then it would not be useful to even discuss this issue. Population estimates for Ephraim and Judah at the time of the division into two nations are not available in the Bible. However, the ratio of Ephraim's population to Judah's can be approximated by using the population estimates for each of the tribes as given in Numbers Chapter 26.

For readers who are not interested in the number crunching to estimate the present-day population of Ephraimite descendants, please go to the end of this section for a summary of the findings.

First, Judah's population is estimated. Benjamin had joined Judah from the very beginning, and according to Joshua 19:1-9, the tribe of Simeon had located within in Judah's land prior to the division, so it is assumed here that all of Simeon is also counted as part of Judah. Also, half of the Levites are assumed to be in Judah, and the other half in Ephraim. Adding these population numbers from Numbers 26 gives the denominator for the Ephraim/Judah ratio. The numerator, then, is just the sum of the remaining tribes that are part of Ephraim.

Thus, at the time of division into two nations, dividing Ephraim's population by Judah's shows that there were about 3.2 times as many Ephraimites as Judites. Multiplying today's Jewish (Judah) population by three would give a rough estimate of today's Ephraimite population (which assumes equal population growth rates, making the estimate even rougher). Unfortunately, it is not this simple.

There are several Bible passages showing that other people within Ephraim's tribes later were also assimilated into Judah, but these passages unfortunately do not indicate numbers.

II Chronicles 11:14-17 states:

> 14For the Levites left their common-lands and their posses-
> sions and came to Judah and Jerusalem, for Jeroboam and his
> sons had rejected them from serving as priests to the LORD.
> 15Then he appointed for himself priests for the high places, for
> the demons, and the calf idols which he had made. 16And after
> *the Levites left*, those from all the tribes of Israel, such as set
> their heart to seek the LORD God of Israel, came to Jerusalem
> to sacrifice to the LORD God of their fathers. 17So they
> strengthened the kingdom of Judah.

Here we see that the Levites joined Judah after Jeroboam, king of the northern kingdom, rejected their priesthood, and some from the various northern tribes who "set their heart to seek the Lord" also joined Judah.

We also see a little later that still more Ephraim people left and joined Judah.

II Chronicles 15:9 states: 9Then he (King Asa of Judah) gathered all Judah and Benjamin, and those who dwelt with them from Ephraim, Manasseh, and Simeon, for they came over to him in great numbers from Israel when they saw that the LORD his God was with him.

"Great numbers" joined Judah when they saw that Yahweh was with Judah. It is, of course, difficult to quantify what "great numbers" really means in terms of the number of people who left Ephraim.

During King Hezekiah's reign, additional people from the northern kingdom left to join Judah. II Chronicles 30:25-26 states:
[25]The whole assembly of Judah rejoiced, also the priests and Levites, all the assembly that came from Israel, the sojourners who came from the land of Israel, and those who dwelt in Judah. [26]So there was great joy in Jerusalem, for since the time of Solomon the son of David, king of Israel, *there had* been nothing like this in Jerusalem.

It is clear from the foregoing that it would not be correct to simply just use a factor of three to multiply the current Jewish population in order to roughly estimate Ephraim's current population. A credible "rough" estimate for Ephraim seems to be impossible given the rather sparse data in the Bible. Therefore, in the interest of at least being conservative, *it is assumed here that Ephraim's and Judah's populations were approximately equal after* the subsequent departures of people who left Ephraim and joined Judah.

Whatever the number, we do know that Ephraim's population had to be very large. Jacob said in Genesis 48:19 that "Ephraim's descendants shall become a multitude of nations." "Multitude" as used in other places in the Hebrew Scriptures always means a *very large* number of people – equivalent to particles of "sand on the seashore." (Hosea 1:10) Therefore, Ephraim's descendants are likely much greater in number than is assumed here.

Further, Josephus described the initial scattering of Israel/Ephraim as "an immense multitude, not to be estimated by numbers" and located "beyond the Euphrates". *(6)* Also, Edersheim confirms that they were scattered in the areas of the Medes and the Euphrates, and that the "biblical account of the deportation of Israel into exile is supplemented and confirmed by the Assyrian records." *(7)* And, Jeremiah 46:28 states that Jacob, which means **Ephraim and Judah**, have been driven to other nations.

If Ephraim's population is assumed roughly equal to the present population of the Jewish people (Judah), we need to find a way to estimate the present Jewish population. This figure will be estimated <u>assuming that the 66-70 Jewish war with the Romans, the Holocaust and the Russian pogroms had not occurred</u>. These three events were all drastic and extraordinary attempts to wipe out the Jewish people, and have been quantified in the historical literature. Assuming that these events had not occurred will provide a more valid estimate, since nothing comparable to them has happened to Ephraim's descendants.

The Jewish historian, Flavius Josephus, in his book *The Wars of the Jews* reported that 1,100,000 Jewish people perished in the war of 66-70. *(8)* It would be very conservative to assume that their descendants could today number 10 million. Not only is 10 million on the low side, but the assumption also does not take account of the 132-135 war, where many more Jewish people were killed.

About six million died in the Holocaust and around a half million to a million died in the Russian pogroms from the 1880s to the early 1900s. If these people had not died, their descendants today would number around 10-15 million (conservatively). So, let's assume that 13 million are added to the 12 million Jewish people alive today (six in U.S., five in Israel, one elsewhere), giving around 25 million Jewish people who would be alive today if the Holocaust and pogroms had not occurred. Adding the 10 million figure from the preceding paragraph to this, gives a total of around 35 million who would be alive today if the war of 66-70, the Holocaust, and the pogroms *had not occurred.*

It is concluded that somewhere between 25 – 50 million Jewish people could be alive today if these three events had not occurred. That this is an extremely conservative estimate is suggested from a syndicated column written by George Will in April 2002: "If the percentage of the world's population that was Jewish in the era of the Roman Empire were Jewish today, there would be 200 million Jews." So, there also could be many millions of gentiles in excess of the 25 – 50 million range.

The point being made here is that tens of millions of Ephraim's descendants are alive today. Whatever the number, it is large. These people are spread all over the world and do not know that they descended from Ephraim because their identity has been lost. Some unknown portion of this 25 – 50 million became gentile Christians. Therefore, answering the question posed at the beginning of this section, it is important that Ephraim/Christianity's physical descendants be accounted for in any discussion of Yahweh's complete restoration of Israel. They are a part of Israel.

For the last 50 or so years, everyone has been concentrating on the return of millions of Judah's descendants (Jews) to the land of Israel, and rightly so. We have seen numerous prophecies fulfilled, as enumerated earlier. However, in the near future, we are likely to also see the return of many of Ephraim's descendants (gentiles) to Israel, and most of them probably will not have any idea why they want to return. They will return because of an inner feeling that "it's the right thing to do". Many Christians feel called to go to Israel as volunteers to work with Christian organizations supporting Israel. Many will recognize that it is Yahweh calling them home.

Only Yahweh knows exactly who these people are and when He will call them back to the land. We may not even be able to recognize that this is happening until the tribes of Israel are reassembled in the Millennium and the land is divided as Yahweh commands in Ezekiel 47:21-23:

> [21]"Thus you shall divide this land among yourselves according to the tribes of Israel. [22]It shall be that you will divide it by lot as an inheritance for yourselves, and for the *strangers* who dwell among you and who bear children among you. They shall be to you as native-born among the children of Israel; they shall have an inheritance with you among the tribes of Israel. [23]And it shall be *that* in whatever tribe the stranger dwells, there you shall give *him* his inheritance," says the Lord GOD. (emphasis added)

We could be surprised and amazed at a future time to see some Christian relatives and friends deciding to pack up and go to Israel. It is likely that the word *"stranger"* in the above verses refers to gentile believers who are not descendants of Ephraim, because gentile believers who are Ephraim's descendants will, under

Yahweh's direction, take their place naturally within their tribe and receive their land inheritance. They will finally be identified in the Millennium.

SUMMARY: Ephraim's population at the time of division into two nations was about three times greater than Judah's. However, an unknown number of Ephraimites were assimilated by Judah before being scattered around the world. Therefore, in the interest of being conservative, Ephraim's population today is assumed to be about the same as Judah's. Judah's population today is estimated to be in the range of 25 to 50 million, assuming that the following events had *not* occurred: the 66-70 war with the Romans, the Russian pogroms, and the Holocaust. Assuming an estimate of 25 to 50 million for Ephraim's descendants today is considered very conservative, because his descendants were predicted "to become a multitude of nations" (Genesis 48:19). A "multitude" in the Bible is equivalent to "sand in the sea". Whatever the number, it is very large, and some portion of these descendants would have become believers. Therefore, answering the question posed at the beginning of this section, it *is important* to account for these people (descendants of Ephraim who became Christians) in any discussion of restoration, because they will be part of future Israel.

REVIEWING THE DISPERSION AND RETURN

The Wheelocks have provided a good summary of the dispersion and return of Israel/Ephraim and Judah/Jews:

"The northern ten tribes of the House of Israel were taken captive in 722 BC and never returned to the land of Israel as a body of people, although a small remnant of them are undoubtedly mixed in with today's Jewish population. The vast majority of the House of Israel have spread around the world. In some cases, they remained together and became known by other names, such as the Shinlung tribe of India and the Anglo-Saxon people of Britain. Still others remained in the vast stretches of Asia, while others migrated into Africa. Eventually, they made their way to the New world and even the islands of the South Pacific. Through intermarriage, the skin color and facial features of those original Israelites have taken on the form of the indigenous people with whom they intermarried, so that today's Israelites can be found among all the people groups of the world. . . As of this date the House of Israel has not yet returned to the land from its captivity, although there are most certainly a few in Israel who are descended from the northern ten tribes. The House of Judah, on the other hand, was not only sent into captivity and returned (during the time of Ezra and Nehemiah), they were dispersed a second time, after the destruction of the Second Temple. They began returning from that dispersion in the late nineteenth century, which culminated in the establishment of the state of Israel in 1948. Nevertheless, the House of Israel will yet return to the land, along with those of the House of Judah who are still in the Diaspora (dispersed around the world): 'He will lift up a banner to the nations from afar, and will whistle to them from the end of the earth; surely they shall come with speed, swiftly' (Isaiah 5:26)" *(9)*

The "banner", of course, is Yeshua (Isaiah 11:10), and, as we have seen, the House of Israel is at least a part of the Christian community, and will be returning to the land. It would be orthwhile to also review Ephesians 2:13-17 again:

> [13]But now in Christ Jesus you who once were far off have been brought near by the blood of Christ.
>
> [14]For He Himself is our peace, who has made both one, and has broken down the middle wall of separation, [15]having abolished in His flesh the enmity, . . . so as to create in Himself one new man *from* the two, *thus* making peace, [16]and that He might reconcile them both to God in one body through the cross, thereby putting to death the enmity. [17]And He came and preached peace to you who were afar off and to those who were near. [18]For through Him we both have access by one Spirit to the Father.

As previously emphasized, this passage connects the coming reunion of the Christians and the Jews. Dr. Douglas Wheeler offers this comment on the above passage:

"So how are we doing? Are Jews and gentiles united, bound,

twisted together, and unified for a specific purpose? There still is a long way for us to go. This passage has only begun to come to pass. A great deal of the church is still anti-Semitic, thinking that the Jews are still under the curse of God and that the church has replaced Israel. A large portion of the church still has no idea that we share a common heritage with Israel. We share the same root. A great portion of the church still teaches the Word of God from a Greek mindset rather a Hebraic mindset." *(10)*

But, what about the numerous Christians who did not descend from Ephraim? What is their status? Yahweh has *somehow* already included these people with Ephraim/Christianity, and they will also be included in the reunion depicted in Ezekiel 37 and Ephesians 2. This has to be the case because, as pointed out earlier, the Bible says that *only two groups of people will be united.* This is a topic of considerable debate and speculation among various authors and Bible scholars. While this is a mystery for now, it will be resolved when the time of the coming reunion is at hand.

Christians in the world today do not know whether they are descendants of Ephraim, and it makes no difference that they do not know. There certainly are not distinctions between groups of Christians. At the time of entering the Millennium, those who are descendants will likely return to their original tribes, and those who are not will either be assimilated into the tribes or go elsewhere. The key to this depends on how Ezekiel 47:21-23 is interpreted. This passage was discussed earlier and is repeated for reference:

> 21"Thus you shall divide this land among yourselves according to the tribes of Israel. 22It shall be that you will divide it by lot as an inheritance for yourselves, and for the strangers who dwell among you and who bear children among you. They shall be to you as native-born among the children of Israel; they shall have an inheritance with you among the tribes of Israel. 23And it shall be *that* in whatever tribe the stranger dwells, there you shall give *him* his inheritance," says the Lord GOD.

One possible interpretation is that the Christian believers who are not descended from Ephraim will have the option of requesting an inheritance in Israel or opting for a place outside of Israel. Another possibility is that Yahweh will want all Christians to be part of Israel, and therefore require that they become "native-born" and receive "an inheritance". Whatever the case, this will not be an issue, because at that time *everyone who is with Yeshua in the Millennial Kingdom will be experiencing unbounded joy, regardless of physical location.*

THE FIRST CENTURY JERUSALEM SYNAGOGUE

The glorious picture of the reunion has also been captured by the recent rediscovery of the first century Judeo-Christian synagogue on Mount Zion, which was discussed earlier, but now in more detail. Recall that in this synagogue was found the Messianic Seal of the Jerusalem Church, re-emerging after nearly 2000 years of burial. A depiction of the Seal, the "grafted in" emblem, is shown on the book cover. Here are some excerpts from a recent book on this subject:

"Although it (the Seal) was carved and painted by the hands of the very first believers, perhaps even by one or more of the twelve apostles themselves, we believe the Messianic Seal proclaims several monumentally important messages . . . we determined to present this book in two parts: Part One, an entirely historical presentation of the events spanning several centuries, leading up to the emergence of the Nazarene Sect of Judaism and ultimately to the Jerusalem Church the Nazarenes established on Mount Zion; Part Two, a biblical interpretation of the Messianic Seal and a suggestion regarding its contemporary implications. . . The Seal, consisting of three parts in a vertical line. . . is deeply significant. The Seal signifies the body of believers (the fish) connected through the stump of Jesse (Star) to the Holy of Holies (Candelabra) and therefore to God. . ." *(11)*

In the context of this book, the Seal shows Christianity (the fish) connected through Hebraic roots (the star of David—stump of Jesse) to the Jewish people (the Menorah). This picture is exactly the same as those described above in Ezekiel 37 and Ephesians 2.

This is the picture of the unity that existed in biblical Christianity prior to 100 AD and that will exist again when Christianity reunites with Judaism. It is also shown on the front cover.

The picture also reminds us of Romans 11, wherein gentile believers are "grafted into" the Hebraic roots of the faith. It is well worthwhile to review Romans 11:17-19:

> [17]And if some of the branches were broken off, and you, being a wild olive tree, were *grafted in* among them, and with them became a partaker of the root and fatness of the olive tree, [18]do not boast against the branches. But if you do boast, *remember that* you do not support the root, but the root supports you. [19]You will say then, "Branches were broken off that I might be *grafted in*." (emphasis added)

"Grafted in" is highlighted in verses 17 and 19 to emphasize that the gentiles have been offered the privilege by Yahweh to be "grafted in" to Israel's olive tree. Those who are grafted in have a responsibility to help the broken off branches, Jewish people who have not recognized Yeshua as their Messiah, be re-grafted in to their own tree.

Dr. John Garr comments on "unity" in this way: "Restoring the Hebraic foundations of Christian faith will of necessity produce a restoration of the unity that characterized the church in the times of Jesus and the apostles. The Hebraic concept of cohesion in diversity that the earliest church modeled will be restored in this the time of the restoration of all things (Acts 3:20-21)." *(12)*

In summary, the important points are emphasized again. When the prophecies in Ezekiel 37 and Ephesians 2 are fulfilled, Christianity and Judaism will finally be united through Yeshua – Jewish and gentile believers will become "one stick", "one new man". Christianity will recognize its Hebrew roots and see that its rejection of the Hebrew Scriptures was a grave error. The Jewish people will finally see that their rejection of Yeshua was also a grave error. To emphasize a point made earlier, He will not return until the Jews accept Him as their Messiah, for as Matthew 23:37-39 states:

> (37) "O Jerusalem, Jerusalem, the one who kills the prophets and stones those who are sent to her! How often I wanted to gather your children together, as a hen gathers her chicks under her wings, but you were not willing! (38) See! Your house is left to you desolate; (39) *for I say to you, you shall see Me no more till you say, 'Blessed is He who comes in the name of the LORD!"* (emphasis added)

Since He will not return until the Jews accept Him as Messiah, and since Christians are asked in Romans 11:11 to make Jewish people jealous of their own Messiah, it would seem that the church should be working hard to undo the false theology and persecution that has caused the 1900 years of separation. *Rejection of the Hebrew Scriptures/Torah is the "false theology" for which the church is responsible.*

The monolithic church does not give any signs yet that she is moving in this direction. Fortunately, Yahweh *is moving* to cause small groups of Christians in the U.S. and around the world to wake up, accept the Torah, and form fellowships and congregations with Jewish believers who have accepted Yeshua. These small groups are going back to biblical Christianity and starting at the point where Yeshua and the apostles left off. They believe literally what the Bible says and therefore reject pagan traditions that are unbiblical.

This chapter has shown that, according to the Bible, Ephraim/Christianity is a subset of Ephraim/Israel; that is, numerous Christians are physical descendants of Ephraim. Not all of Ephraim's descendants became Christians, and not all Christians are physical descendants of Ephraim. But, the Bible is clear in stating that Ephraim's "descendants shall become a multitude of nations". From this multitude have come many Christians.

It must be stressed that this glorious reunion is limited to those descendants of Ephraim and Judah who have accepted Yeshua as Lord and Savior. Those from Ephraim and Judah who have rejected Him will also be rejected from receiving salvation and eternal life.

9. SUMMARY and CONCLUDING COMMENTS

Brief Summary:

- The church changed Yahweh's 7th day Sabbath to Sunday
- The church changed Yahweh's Passover to a day honoring the goddess Easter
- The church observes Yeshua's birthday on the date of a pagan god's birthday
- The church does not observe Yahweh's Leviticus 23 appointments
- Many in the church believe that the church has replaced Israel in Yahweh's plan
- Many in the church are anti-Semitic
- There are other deviations from biblical Christianity that have not been addressed herein

WHY?? Because the church has disregarded Yahweh's Hebrew Scriptures/Torah

Expanded Summary:

The early Christian church became separated from its Hebrew roots as a result of the efforts of some early "church fathers", leaders taking over after Jesus and the apostles were gone, to distance the church from Judaism. The "church fathers" thought they had better ideas than Yeshua for organizing and leading this new religion, Christianity. Anti-Semitism became one of their main weapons in the effort to distance the church from the Jews.

The pagan influence of the religion Mithraism, which was competing with Christianity in the early centuries, also was responsible for this separation. Mithraism harbored many pagan rites and traditions that had come into existence in the ancient past, and many "church fathers" became heavily influenced by them. The net impact was the blending of men's traditions and paganism with true biblical belief, taking Christianity away from the purely biblical path laid out by Yahweh and Yeshua. By embracing paganism, the early church leaders were able to greatly increase church membership among the gentiles. They could still hang on to their pagan rites, because these rites had now become "christianized".

The forced separation, the influence of Mithraism, and vicious anti-Semitism are all still haunting the church today, and these anti-biblical opponents are primarily responsible for the church's rejection of the Hebrew Scriptures/Torah. The church today is blinded to its need to spiritually apply the Hebrew Scriptures/Torah, because it has been disconnected from its Hebrew roots. Christians do not understand that, while Yahweh's Torah includes the "law", it more importantly also includes His invaluable teachings and instructions. The church has hidden the teaching aspect of the Torah ever since the early centuries.

Rejecting the Torah has caused the church to accept the non-biblical substitutions of Sunday for the Sabbath and Easter for Passover. It has further caused Christians to view Yahweh's Leviticus 23 appointments as "Jewish things" that can be ignored. The truth of the matter is that they are not "Jewish things", and Yahweh has invited gentiles to participate in these appointments, promising joy in doing so. By ignoring His appointments, Christians have lost a wonderful way to commemorate what Yeshua has already done for us, and to rehearse and anticipate the joy of what He will do for us when He returns.

However, even with the covering up of the truth of the Torah, there yet remains optimism and hope as Yahweh's divine plan comes to fruition. The Bible clearly shows that many of Ephraim's descendants were scattered and assimilated around the world in the same way Judah's descendants (Jews) were scattered. However, while the Jewish people have maintained their identity in the face of continual tribulation through the centuries, Ephraim's descendants became "not a people" and completely lost their identity. Phase I of Israel's restoration, which is the return of the Jews to the land, is well underway. Phase II of her restoration, which is the return of Ephraim's descendants, is just starting. When these two phases have been completed, Yahweh's final restoration of Israel will be at hand.

Who are the descendants of Ephraim? After all, the Bible says that Ephraim's "descendants shall become a multitude of nations"(Genesis 48:19), so it seems important to inquire about this "multitude". The Bible says in Ezekiel Chapter 37, and in many passages building up to it, that there will be a future reunion between Ephraim and Judah. It was also shown that many Christians have descended from Ephraim, and that the reunion in Ezekiel 37 is actually between the Christians and Jews. This is the same reunion that Yeshua describes in Ephesians Chapter 2.

By the time the reunion takes place, in fulfillment of Ezekiel 37 and Ephesians 2, Christians will have accepted the Hebrew Scriptures/Torah, and the Jews will have accepted Yeshua as Lord and Savior. However, the descendants of Ephraim and Judah who have rejected Yeshua are not part of the reunion. A biblical understanding of these seminal events has been lost to the church because of not seeing spiritual applications in the Hebrew Scriptures/Torah, and lost to the Jews because of not seeing that Yeshua is their Messiah.

The recent archeological discovery of the 1st century Jerusalem Church (the biblical church) shows the unity of the early Jewish and gentile believers. For the next 19 centuries after this, the church and Judaism became separated for the many reasons given, and will remain separated until the future reconciliation through Yeshua. The fulfillments of Ezekiel 37 and Ephesians 2 will once again reunite biblical Christianity and Judaism. The front cover depicts the story of the initial unity of the 1st century church, the separation during following centuries, and then the future reunion.

Christian leaders today frequently promote revival. It would seem, however, that real Yahweh-inspired revival means that the *church* needs to acknowledge and turn from past errors. Unless this happens, why would Yahweh sponsor revival of a church that incorporates pagan traditions? Limited revivals may occur from time to time, but it seems unlikely that a large-scale revival can take place unless it is based entirely on *biblical truth.*

Christians who are serious about following the Bible need to ask themselves some important questions:

O Given that the early "church fathers" and Mithraism led the church away from *biblical* Christianity, is it not reasonable to believe that some important biblical passages have been changed or ignored?

O With the understanding that "law" in the English translations of the Bible is actually the "Torah"(law, teachings, instructions) from the Hebrew Scriptures, does this not mean that Christians need to re-evaluate the Torah to determine how it relates to them?

O Yahweh commanded that the 7th day Sabbath be kept holy (Genesis 2:3, Exodus 20:8), and this was obeyed throughout the Hebrew Scriptures; and then obeyed by Yeshua, the apostles and the 1st century Christian church. When Yeshua returns, the Sabbath will again be honored as Yahweh's holy day of rest throughout the Millennium (Ezekiel 40-48). Who authorized the substitution of Sunday for the Sabbath during the "church age" only?

O The same question applies concerning the substitution of Easter for Passover.
Who authorized the substitution of Easter for Passover during the "church age" only?

O Yahweh gave us His other appointments (feasts) in Leviticus

23 that were observed throughout the Hebrew Scriptures and by Yeshua in the 1st century, and will be observed again in the Millennium. Who authorized the abandonment of Yahweh's appointments during the "church age" only?

MESSIANIC FELLOWSHIPS

Many Messianic believers, both Jewish and gentile, are returning to a Torah-based foundation, which includes following the New Testament, and observing the Sabbath, Passover, the Leviticus 23 appointments, and other biblical commandments in accordance with the Bible. Many Messianic fellowships and congregations are being organized and led by lay believers. They are forming around the world, and reflect the growing awareness of the need for unity between the brothers, Ephraim/Christianity and Judah/Jews. These fellowships are microcosms of the unity present in the 1st century church and the reunion that is coming. Yahweh seems now to be moving rapidly to fulfill the prophecies implicit in Ezekiel 37 and Ephesians 2.

Many of these Messianic fellowships have more gentile members than Jewish ones. One reason for this may be that gentiles are awakening to the Torah, and are therefore reaching out to the Jewish people in an attempt to try and make up for the centuries of Christian-sponsored persecution. They are seeing their Hebraic roots in Romans Chapter 11, and are trying to fulfill the admonition in Romans 11:11 "to provoke them (Jews) to jealousy"— making the Jews jealous of their own Messiah. The fellowships normally attempt to recapture much of the culture and language that were present during 1st century biblical times. The emphasis is to create an environment in which Jewish believers feel comfortable and know that they are accepted, and to see that their culture is intact. These Messianic believers – Jewish and gentile – are trying to worship Yahweh and Yeshua according to *biblical* Christianity as established by Yeshua in the 1st century.

APPENDIX A

THE DESCENDANTS OF ISHMAEL AND ESAU

The godly line of Abraham-Isaac-Jacob/Israel, and in particular the tribes of Judah (Jews) and Ephraim, have been the primary topics discussed in the text. But, what about Ishmael, Isaac's brother, and Esau, Jacob/Israel's brother? What happened to them and where did their descendants go? It is of interest to at least briefly try to answer these questions, particularly in view of today's world events. Perhaps even more important than their destinations, however, is to see that Ishmael and Esau were the actual seeds of the *anti-Semitism that is consuming the Arab world today.*

In Genesis 16:10-12, Yahweh's angel tells Hagar, Ishmael's mother, that her descendants will be too numerous to count. The angel also gives some clues as to what type of man Ishmael will be:

> [10]Then the Angel of the LORD said to her, "I will multiply your descendants exceedingly, so that they shall not be counted for multitude." [11]And the Angel of the LORD said to her: "Behold, you *are* with child, And you shall bear a son. You shall call his name Ishmael, Because the LORD has heard your affliction. [12]He shall be a wild man; His hand *shall be* against every man, And every man's hand against him. And he shall dwell in the presence of all his brethren."

Genesis 25:18 says that the multitude of Ishmael's descendants settled in areas mainly to the east and south of Israel:

> [17]These *were* the years of the life of Ishmael: one hundred and thirty-seven years; and he breathed his last and died, and was gathered to his people. [18]They (his descendants) dwelt from Havilah as far as Shur, which *is* east of Egypt as you go toward Assyria. He died in the presence of all his brethren.

The area from Havilah to Shur includes the present-day nations of Syria and Saudi Arabia.

In Genesis 26: 23 Yahweh said to Isaac's wife, Rebekah, that the two nations descending from Isaac and Ishmael will be separated, meaning antagonism right from the start:

> [23]And the LORD said to her: "Two nations *are* in your womb, Two peoples shall be separated from your body; *One* people shall be stronger than the other, And the older shall serve the younger."

Putting the above passages together, it is seen that Ishmael (and descendants) would be very difficult to get along with, continually fighting among themselves and others, and would inhabit lands around Israel. Esau also had numerous numerous descendants (Genesis 36), and the last verse states that Esau was the father of the Edomites. Present-day Jordan includes Edom within its boundaries.

Thus, Ishmael's and Esau's descendants would occupy the above three Arab nations, and they likely would have also settled in other present-day Arab countries. Ishmael had early in childhood "mocked" Isaac and Esau had vowed to kill Jacob. Esau had also married pagan wives to spite Isaac and Rebekah, his parents, who had asked him specifically to not marry pagan women. These events could also reflect Ishmael's and Esau's deep jealousy that Isaac and Jacob were given the divine promises. These events initiated the Arab hatred for Israel that rages on today, which is the beginning of anti-Semitism. The Islam terrorists attacking Israel and the U.S. today are descended from Ishmael and Esau.

IS GOD OF THE BIBLE, YAHWEH, THE SAME AS ALLAH?

In the media we frequently hear the name "God" and "Allah" being used, with the implication that the two names are interchangeable. What is the truth of the matter? Is "God" really Allah? This is a critical issue for both believers and unbelievers. We all need to know the TRUTH.

To illustrate the confusion, The Sacramento Bee on 10/24/02 published a first page article to be on high alert for a possible terrorist attack in Sacramento the next day. The article included this statement: "The message the FBI received appeared to have come in some sort of text, with the phrases 'may God protect Islam' and 'may God destroy America.'"

Is this the God of the Bible . . . or could this be Allah?

One more example: The Auburn (California) Journal on 10/25/02 contained an article entitled, "Muslims brace again for public backlash", referring to the arrest of a Muslim man in connection with the sniper shootings. The article went on to say: "The whole Muslim community was praying day and night: 'God, please. There has to be no connection to Muslims', Faiz Rehman of the American Muslim Council said Thursday."

Is this really the God of the Bible . . . or could this be Allah?

Beyond any doubt, *THE GOD OF THE BIBLE, YAHWEH, AND ALLAH ARE NOT THE SAME*, and have no relationship with each other whatsoever. Whenever a Muslim individual or organization uses "God" he means "Allah". Here's why this is the case.

God of the Bible, Yahweh, promised Abraham that He would make both of his sons, Isaac and Ishmael, into great nations. In the Book of Genesis, Yahweh said that multitudes would descend from his two sons, and today millions of Jews (from Judah) and Christians (from Ephraim) are descendants of Isaac, and over one billion Muslims are descendants of Ishmael

While Genesis makes it clear that both Isaac and Ishmael would father great nations, He also said very clearly *that the godly (divine) line goes through Isaac only.* Yahweh said that from Isaac and his son Jacob would come peoples, land, and the promised seed,

Yeshua. Ishmael, and later Esau, were both promised multitudes of people and great amounts of land, *but not the divine blessing.* In Genesis 17:19-22, Yahweh states:

> [19] . . . "Sarah your wife shall bear you a son, and you shall call his name Isaac; I will establish My covenant with him for an everlasting covenant, *and* with his descendants after him. [20]And as for Ishmael, I have heard you. Behold, I have blessed him, and will make him fruitful, and will multiply him exceedingly. He shall beget twelve princes, and I will make him a great nation. [21]But My covenant I will establish with Isaac, whom Sarah shall bear to you at this set time next year."

The rest of the Bible after Genesis deals only with Isaac's descendants (Israel) in the Hebrew Scriptures and the story of Christianity in the New Testament.

In the 7th century Islam became the religion of Ishmael's and Esau's descendants (mainly the Arabs), when it was created by Muhammad. He later selected Allah as Islam's deity. Allah, the moon god, was one of 360 idols worshiped by Islam before Muhammad chose Allah to be "the god". It's interesting that Yahweh created the earth and man, and yet in Islam Muhammad created his "god".

Therefore, we can see just from the discussion so far, that the God of the Bible, Yahweh, and Allah are distinct and separate deities. But let's look at some additional factors. First, Islam's Koran (9:5) states: ". . . fight and slay the infidels wherever ye find them, seize them, and beleaguer them." The Koran, which is Islam's bible, includes Jews and Christians as 'infidels'. This alone proves that Yahweh and Allah are completely different. Yahweh obviously never said or intimated in the Bible to "fight and slay the Jews and Christians", because they are His people whom He created.

Yahweh *did command* His people, Israel, to wipe out the Canaanites and other pagans when Israel entered the Promised Land under Joshua in around 1400 BC. Yahweh commanded Israel to completely wipe them out because of their gross immorality, which included child sacrifice to their idols and gods (this should give us cause us to pause for a moment and ask, "what will He do to the U.S. since we have sacrificed 40 million babies through abortion?").

The Koran emphatically denies the divine nature of Yeshua, and denies that He is the Son of Yahweh. It also makes abundantly clear that Muhammad is Allah's Prophet. If Allah and Yahweh are the same, why isn't Muhammad mentioned in the Bible?

Also, a centerpiece of Islam is "jihad" (holy war) in the name of Allah. Where does God or the Bible ever mention "jihad"? If Yahweh and Allah are the same, surely "jihad" or its equivalent would be in the Bible.

That God of the Bible, Yahweh, and Allah are not the same is also verified by a number of additional comments from others, two of which are:

o A Palestinian Arab and noted scholar, Dr. Anis Shorrosh, stated categorically that "The Allah of the Koran is not the same as the God of the Bible."

o Allah is a purely Arabic term used in reference to an Arabian deity. The origin of this goes back to pre-Moslem times. Allah is not a common name meaning "God". (*The Islamic Invasion*, Robert Morley)"

Yahweh has permitted the Arab terrorism of Israel because of her repeated disobedience as Deuteronomy 28:66-67 shows:

> [66]Your life shall hang in doubt before you; you shall fear day and night, and have no assurance of life. [67]In the morning you shall say, 'Oh, that it were evening!' And at evening you shall say, 'Oh, that it were morning!' because of the fear which terrifies your heart, and because of the sight which your eyes see.

In some Bible versions "fear" in this passage is replaced by "terror", so Yahweh actually predicted the terror that has come to haunt Israel, and more recently the U.S.

It has been shown in this book that Yahweh completely restores

Israel, which will end in the reunion of Judah (Jews) and Ephraim(gentiles and Christians). But what is the final disposition of the Arabs? Their fate is utter destruction, unless they come to faith in Yeshua. Obadiah 18 states:

> [18]The house of Jacob shall be a fire, And the house of Joseph a
> flame; But the house of Esau *shall be* stubble;
> They shall kindle them and devour them, And no survivor shall
> *remain* of the house of Esau,"
> For the LORD has spoken.

The verses leading up to v. 18 showed Yahweh's displeasure at how Esau had mistreated his brother Jacob (Israel) through the centuries and had rejoiced over Israel's captivities and other hardships. Thus, in the end, Yahweh completely destroys the house of Esau, and it is likely that many from the house of Ishmael will suffer the same fate.

However, some Arab nations will actually come to faith in Yeshua, and end up being a blessing to Israel (Isaiah 19:19-25, 60:6-7). It is remarkable that after centuries of persecution of Israel, some Arab nations will come to salvation through Yeshua!

Behold, how good and how pleasant *it is f*or brethren to dwell together in unity! (Psalm 133:1)

GLOSSARY

ARMAGEDDON –The final battle between Israel and the other nations of the world at which time Yahweh (God) sends Yeshua (Jesus) to destroy the armies attacking Israel. Yeshua then takes believers into His Millennium Kingdom here on earth.

ANTI-SEMITISM – is the intolerance and hatred of the Jewish people through the millennia. It started in the ancient times of Ishmael and Esau, and developed to major proportions as the early "church fathers" changed biblical Christianity into Catholicism.

BIBLICAL CHRISTIANITY – The Christianity that follows exactly the biblical path laid out by Yeshua and His apostles. Strictly avoids the pagan influences from surrounding cultures that infected the church after Yeshua and the apostles were gone.

BIBLICAL JUDAISM – Biblical Judaism believes and follows the Hebrew Scriptures that are based on the Bible, whereas Rabbinic Judaism is both based on the Bible and the writings of rabbis. It does not accept the New Testament, or Yeshua as the Messiah.

CAUGHT UP – 1 Thessalonians 4:17 says: "After that, we who are still alive and are left will be *caught up* together with them in the clouds to meet the Lord in the air." When the Bible was translated into the Latin Vulgate, *caught up* was translated as "rapture". Rapture is the term that has endured to describe the wonderful event that will occur in the future when Yeshua returns to take believers to heaven (1 Thess 4:16-17, 1 Cor 15:51-53)

CHRISTIAN BELIEVER – is a person who has accepted Yeshua as Lord and Savior, but does not follow spiritual applications in the Hebrew Scriptures/Torah.

CHURCH – The institution that unfortunately allowed some "church fathers" to blend pagan rites from other religions and cultures with biblical Christianity. By around 400 AD, the church had been taken over by Catholicism (a blending of biblical Christianity with paganism). After the Protestant Reformation in the 16th century, some of the paganism was eliminated, but the church has retained much of it to this day.

CHURCH AGE – is the period between Yeshua's establishment of the church in the 1st century and the time of His second coming.

CHURCH FATHERS – The political and religious men who were leading Christianity between 100 to 500 AD. In general, they were responsible for accelerating anti-Semitism and the separation of Christianity and Judaism.

EPHRAIM – One of the 12 tribes of Israel. Ephraim became the dominant tribe of the northern kingdom of Israel/Ephraim when Israel divided into two nations (Ephraim and Judah) around 930 BC. After the division, Israel and Ephraim are names denoting the same nation.

EPHRAIM/ISRAEL – Denotes that "Ephraim" and "Israel" refer to the northern kingdom (nation) of Israel after the division around 930 BC into the two kingdoms.

EPHRAIM/CHRISTIANITY – Denotes that through the centuries a large number of Christians have descended from Ephraim, who was the father of "a multitude of nations". (Genesis 48:19)

GENTILE – While there are some differences between the meaning of "gentile" and "non-Jewish", for the purposes of the way these terms are used in this book, these differences have no bearing. Thus, the terms are used interchangeably.

HEBREW ROOTS – are the biblical foundations of Christianity starting with the ancient Hebrews and continuing through biblical Judaism. Biblical Judaism is also the mother of biblical Christianity.

HEBREW SCRIPTURES – are generally the same as the Old Testament, except the OT contains some mistranslations and the order of the books is different. The major error was converting "Torah" or "teaching" into the single word "law" in the OT.

JEWISH BELIEVER – A person who practices Judaism, believing in Yahweh and in the Hebrew Scriptures/Torah, but does not believe in the New Testament or in Yeshua as the Messiah.

JEWISH CHRISTIAN – A Jewish believer in Yeshua

JEWS – Descendants of the nation of Judah and descendants from the other Hebrew tribes who became assimilated into Judah.

JUDAH – The tribe from whom Yeshua descended. It also became known as the southern kingdom of Judah when Israel divided into two nations around 930 BC.

JUDAISM – The worship of Yahweh through the Hebrew Scriptures. Judaism does not accept the New Testament or that Yeshua is the Messiah.

MESSIANIC BELIEVER– means believers, Jewish or gentile, who believe in the Messiah, Yeshua.

MILLENNIAL KINGDOM – is the 1000 year period that immediately follows Yeshua's second coming (see Ezekiel 40-48, Zechariah 14 and Revelation 20).

MITHRAISM – An ancient religion that preceded Christianity. Worship was built around a sun god, and many of the pagan traditions and rites from Mithraism were blended with biblical Christianity. It competed with Christianity during the early centuries, and was the religion of the Roman Emperors, the army, and many in the Roman Empire. Mithraism was a forerunner of Catholicism.

PRESENT AGE – started at Yeshua's first coming and ends when He returns and establishes His Millennial Kingdom.

PRE-TRIBULATION RAPTURE VIEW – The view that the rapture (caught up) will occur before or at the beginning of the seven year tribulation period. Believers will not have to suffer any of the tribulation during the seven year period.

PRE-WRATH RAPTURE – The view that the rapture (caught up) will occur approximately three fourths of the way through the seven year tribulation period, which marks the time when Yahweh starts bringing His wrath on earth. Believers will have to suffer tribulation in the form of man's wrath, but will be raptured before Yahweh's wrath.

RAPTURE – See "caught up"

SEPTUAGINT – Translation of the Hebrew Scriptures into Greek around 300 to 200 BC.

SEVEN YEAR TRIBULATION PERIOD – is the seven year period of tribulation which starts after the Anti-Christ (Daniel 9, Matthew 24, 1 Thessalonians 5) comes into power and ends with Yeshua's return.

TORAH-BASED LIFESTYLE – The perfect model of the Torah-based lifestyle is Yeshua Himself. One of the major doctrines of the New Testament is for believers to be like Him – to try and emulate what He does. To do this, we need to obey, as best we can, the same teachings and commandments that He obeyed, which are none other than the Hebrew Scriptures/Torah. The New Covenant states clearly that, for both Jewish and non-Jewish believers, Yahweh will put His Torah "in their minds and write them on their hearts." (Jeremiah 31:31-34; Hebrews 8:7-12) The foundation, or beginning, of a Torah-based lifestyle is to observe the Sabbath and Yahweh's Leviticus 23 appointments, because doing so follows specific biblical teachings and commands that Yeshua obeyed. As believers grow spiritually, they can add to this foundation by striving to be obedient in other areas where Yeshua demonstrated His Torah-based lifestyle.

STRONG'S – Exhaustive Concordance provides definitions and meanings for nearly every word in the Bible, and its numbering system links it to Hebrew and Greek dictionaries.

TORAH – The first five books of the Bible. But Torah can also refer to all of the Hebrew Scriptures. In this book Torah and Hebrew Scriptures are used interchangeably.

YAHWEH (GOD) – In Exodus 3:14-15 (The Tanakh — the Jewish Bible) we see God formally naming himself *Yahweh*, a name deriving from the four letter Hebrew Tetragrammaton (hey-waw-hey-yod). The four letters transliterate in English to YHWH. Numerous pagan "gods" have come out of the different nations. It is fitting here to use the actual name of the real one and only God of the universe – His name is *Yahweh.*

YESHUA (JESUS) – Yeshua is His Hebrew name, the name His mother would have called Him. The original Hebrew form was *Yehoshuah* ("Yahweh is Salvation"). *Yeshua* obviously derives from the Hebrew form by simply dropping the "ho" and then the final "h". It is fitting here to use His Hebrew/Jewish Name to continually remind us that our Savior is Jewish – His name is *Yeshua.*

CHAPTER ENDNOTES

CHAPTER 1 INTRODUCTION

1. *The Essential Catholic Handbook*, Liguori Publications, 1997, p. 210

CHAPTER 2 SEPARATION OF CHRISTIANITY AND JUDAISM

1. Marvin R. Wilson, *Our Father Abraham*, Eerdman's Publishing Co, 1989, pp. 92-93
2. Ray Pritz, Personal Interview, Jerusalem, 1999
3. Wilson, op. sit., p. 93
4. John Chryostom, *The Fathers of the Church*, Catholic University Press, Vol. 68,1979
5. Richard Booker, *Torah: Law or Grace*, 2001
6. John Kennedy, *The Torch of the Testimony*, Seed Sowers Press, 1965, p. 99
7. Charles Bryant-Abraham, *The Residue of Marcionism*, RESTORE! Magazine, Restoration Foundation, Spring 2000, p. 29
8. Jesse L. Hurlbut, *The Story of the Christian Church*, Holt-Rinehart-Winston, 1918, pp. 58-62
9. Justo L. Gonzalez, *The Story of Christianity*, Prince Press, 1984, p. 129

10. Eusebius, *Ecclesiastical History*, Hendrickson Pub, 1998, pp. 423-425
11. Ibid., pp. 182-184
12. Kennedy, op. sit., p. 75
13. Gonzalez, op. sit., p. 122
14. Kennedy, op. sit., pp. 88-89
15. John D. Garr, *Restoring Our Lost Legacy*, Golden Key Books, 1989, p. 22
16. Dave Hunt, *A Woman Rides the Beast*, Harvest House, 1994, p.158
17. Christopher O'Quin, *The Fiscus Judaicus*, Bikurei Tziyon, First Fruits of Zion, Issue 72, 2002, p. 28

CHAPTER 3   THE RELIGION MITHRAISM AND
            ANTI-SEMITISM

1. Lew White, *Fossilized Customs*, 2001, p. 46
2. Geoffrey Parrinder,ed., *World Religions*, Hamlyn Publishing, 1971, p. 187
3. Don Esposito, *The Great Falling Away*, Morris Publishing, 2001, p. 5
4. *Origin of Mithraic Mysteries*, Oxford, New York, 1989
5. David Fingrut, *Mithraism*, An Essay, Internet 2001
6. *From Sabbath to Sunday*, Pontifical Gregorian University Press, Rome, 1977
7. Curtis, Lang, and Petersen, *The 100 Most Important Events in Christian History*, Baker Books, 1998, p. 13
8. Robert Smith, *World Book Encyclopedia*, 2000
9. Author Unknown, Internet, 2002
10. Marvin R. Wilson, *Our Father Abraham*, Eerdman's Publishing, 1989, p. 100
11. Dave Hunt, *The Woman Rides a Beast*, Harvest House, 1994, p. 22-23
12. Levitt Letter, Vol 24, November 2002, p. 3
13. John Garr, *Our Lost Legacy*, Golden Key Books, p. 215
14. Zola Levitt, *Personal Letter to subscribers*, December 2002

15. Ramon Bennett, *Saga: Israel and the Demise of Nations*, Arm of Salvation, 1993, p. x-xi

CHAPTER 4. THE TRUTH ABOUT THE TORAH

1. Marvin R. Wilson, *Our Father Abraham*, Eerdman's Publishing, 1989, pp. 96-97
2. David Friedman, *They Loved the Torah*, Lederer Books, 2001, p. vi
3. Frederick Schweitzer, Judaism – *A Basis for Christian Unity*, RESTORE! Magazine, Restoration Foundation, p. 16
4. Ariel and D'vorah Berkowitz, *Torah Rediscovered*, First Fruits of Zion, 1996, p. 7
5. Jay P. Green, ed., *The Interlinear Hebrew – Greek – English Bible*, Hendrickson Publishers, 1985
6. Philip Yancey, *The Bible Jesus Read*, Zondervan Publishing, 1999, p. 25

CHAPTER 5.   THE TRUTH ABOUT THE SABBATH & INTRODUCTION TO LEV 23

1. John Garr, *Our Lost Legacy*, Golden Key Books, 1989
2. Philip Schaff, *History of the Christian Church*, Eerdman's Publishing, 1910, pp. 202-203
3. Jesse L. Hurlbut, *The Story of the Christian Church*, Zondervan, 1918, p. 36
4. Christopher O'Quin, *Sabbath*, Bikurei Tziyon, Issue 74, First Fruits of Zion, Israel, 2002
5. Charles Buck, *A Theological Dictionary*. "Sabbath"
6. Harold Lindell (editor), *Christianity Today*, November 5, 1976

CHAPTER 6. THE TRUTH ABOUT YAHWEH'S LEVITICUS 23 APPOINTMENTS

1. John Garr, *Our Lost Legacy*, Golden Key Books, 1989, p. 144
2. *The Essential Catholic Handbook*, Liguori Publications, 1997, p.156
3. Pastor George Udvary, *Christmas and the Faith of Our Fathers,* Latter-Days Sentinel, Nov-Dec 02
4. *Birthday of the Son*, Yahweh Restoration Ministry, 2002, pp. 4-9

CHAPTER 7. THE RESTORATION OF ISRAEL – FIRST PHASE

1. David Ettinger, "Israel: The Apple of God's Eye", Zion's Fire, Oct 02, p.12

CHAPTER 8. THE RESTORATION OF ISRAEL – SECOND PHASE

1. Eddie Chumney, *Restoring the Two Houses of Israel*, Serenity Books, 1999
2. Batya Wootten, *Who Is Israel*, Key of David Publishing, 1998
3. Dean and Susan Wheelock, *Abraham's Math*, Hebrew Roots, Issue 02-2, pp. 17-24
4. John MacArthur, *The MacArthur Study Bible*, Word Bibles, 1997
5. William Hendriksen, *Survey of the Bible*, Baker Books, 1976, p. 54
6. William Whiston, *The Works of Josephus*, Hendrickson Publishers, 1987, p. 294
7. Alfred Edersheim, *Bible History*, Hendrickson Publishers, 1995, pp. 905-906
8. Whiston, op. sit., p. 749
9. Wheelock, op. sit., pp. 21-23

10. Douglas Wheeler, *The Echad of God*, RESTORE! Magazine, Restoration Foundation, 2002, p. 85
11. Reuven Schmalz and Raymond Fisher, *The Messianic Seal of the Jerusalem Church*, Olim Publications, Israel, 2001
12. John Garr, *One Ark or Ten Thousand Canoes*, RESTORE! Magazine, Restoration Foundation, 2002, p. 85

Printed in the United States
95607LV00001B/374/A